“You will personally be inspired by P
by Design! In a very honest account, they share their longing to adopt two Cambodian orphans, the agonizing roadblocks, the answered prayers, and a faith in God that should challenge every believer. As adoptive parents ourselves, we highly recommend this book!”

—Josh and Dottie McDowell
Authors and adoptive parents

“*Daughters by Design* is just that, an amazing, faith-filled journey of how a couple willingly followed God’s design, not man’s; trusted the Lord to show them the way; welcomed two young Cambodian girls into their lives; overcame enormous hurdles; and finally adopted them—two daughters by *God’s* design.”

—Judy Long, M.A.L.S.
Head Librarian, Grace International School, Thailand

“My wife and I huddled over a computer on a commuter flight, each vying for a better position to read this wild and holy story. We wept. And by the time we finished, we were exhausted. It is a heartbreaking, impossible adventure that called us to ask the question: are we willing to wait and see the goodness of God?

“But more than exhaustion or tears, we felt awe and gratitude to know this family and their amazing story. We know they are remarkable and normal, amazing and ordinary. They simply don’t see their faithfulness as anything other than what anyone who loves Jesus would do.

“Yet, their extraordinary faithfulness calls me to dream redemption for others, in ways that seem beyond my capacity. But it is not.

“And this glorious book allows us to see how those who dream redemption for others are themselves redeemed by the beauty of love. I love this family. I love their story.

“Most, I love the God who is revealed through the faces of Sivy, Sophie, Paul, and Paula.”

—Dan B. Allender, Ph.D.
professor and founding president Mars Hill Graduate School and
author of *The Wounded Heart* and *Leading with a Limp*

"Paul and Paula Jarot's life is an exemplifying testimony of the love of God for others, specifically for Sivy and Sophie, as they walked this miraculous journey of love and faith that is lived out in this book.

"It brings to us a powerful, vivid, living example of the words of Jesus recorded in Matthew 25:40, 'I tell you the truth, whatever you did for one of the least of these—you did it for me.'"

—Ken Boland
Retired pastor, international school instructor

"I'm so glad this story has been written down! The first time I heard Paula share their adoption story, I reacted, like so many others: "You've gotta write a book!"

"The Psalmist said, 'God puts the lonely in families.' You can trace the hand of God in this story and celebrate His watchful care over two very special orphan girls and the blessing they have become to two very unsuspecting but willing parents.

"Paul and Paula inspired us to follow God on a similar path, welcoming a Thai daughter, when we are old enough to be grandparents. We're grateful that they had already forged this path. And in so doing, they gave us the courage to move forward with our adoption. So, read their book with caution. There's no telling how this family's story might inspire you."

—Matthew and Molly Veldt
Adoptive parents

"It's an amazing and barely conceivable story of international adoption challenges to build a 'second' family. I couldn't put it down. But keep a box of tissue handy—the persistent hope and love shown here will grab your heart and shake you to the core!"

—Penny Lent
Contributing author in Max Lucado's bestseller
It's Not About Me, Teen Edition

Daughters by Design

"As adoptive parents ourselves, we highly recommend this book." –Josh & Dottie McDowell

Daughters by Design

The Miracle Adoption of Two Cambodian Orphans

Paula Jarot

Published by Redemption Press, PO Box 427, Enumclaw, WA 98022.

The author of this book has waived the publisher's suggested editing and proof reading services. As such, the author is responsible for any errors found in this finished product.

ISBN 13: 978-1-63232-754-3
Library of Congress Catalog Card Number: 2010941261

Dedicated to Paul, faithful husband and father,
who obeyed the Designer

Content

Acknowledgments xi

1. Normal is Over 1
2. Timely Detour 5
3. The One in Pink 9
4. Piece by Piece 13
5. Arrival in Cambodia 15
6. Double Blessing 21
7. The Girls Remember 27
8. Sovereign Timing 31
9. So Many Firsts 35
10. Unconditional Love 47
11. They Are Here Now 51
12. The Gift of Language 55
13. Summer Sadness, Summer Gladness 59
14. Pet Parade 65
15. Provision and Protection 69
16. A Daughter's Forgiveness 97
17. A Thankful Heart 99

18. A Tiny Step Forward 103
19. Call Me Sophie 105
20. First Trip Back 109
21. Miracle. 117
22. God Opens the Door 121
23. Great Joy, Deep Grief. 123
24. Back to the Village 127
25. Walk Where Sophie Walked 135
26. The Truth Sets You Free 139
27. Cambodian Adoption. 145
28. Girls Give Praise. 151
29. Mountains of Paperwork 153
30. And the Tears Fell. 157
31. Community of Prayer. 161
32. Forms and More Forms 165
33. The Whole Truth 171
34. Run the Race 177

Epilogue. 183
About the Author 185

Acknowledgments

I WANT TO thank Pam Davis. She walked with me through all the tears and trials of mothering adopted girls. Her God-given ability to counsel my family without an appointment brought healing and strength to our lives. She walked the streets of Phnom Penh, wept in the dump while the children played, and slept on the floor of a village house with me. I thank Pam for loving me from the inside out and guiding my family to healthy relationships. God gave me the girls, but not without a friend and counselor who was willing and able to help me through the rough moments.

Many thanks to Judy Long, who read and reread my manuscript. Judy encouraged me to keep going. She traveled with me to Cambodia and shared personally with the kids who were left in the orphanage. Judy was not afraid to venture into the uncomfortable parts of Cambodia, in order to help me edit my manuscript.

Many thanks to Penny Lent for all the encouragement during the final edits and for sharing her professional expertise.

To the staff at Grace International School, Chiang Mai, Thailand: I thank you. You covered us in prayer from the very beginning of this process. Many people did things "above and beyond the call of duty" to help us along the way. Needed paperwork, extra help with school lessons, and loving patience were given to our girls. Paul and I could not have raised the girls without the help of our Grace family.

And to Paul, my husband and best friend, I thank you. You are everything to me, and without your faithful obedience to the Lord, we would not have these two precious daughters. Thank you for being the Daddy that every little girl needs!

Chapter 1

Normal is Over

THEY CAME WITHOUT suitcases. One wore borrowed shoes that needed to be sent back to the orphanage after she arrived. The other never had owned a doll or slept on a bed.

On Christmas night, 2004, two Cambodian orphans arrived at our home in Chiang Mai, Thailand, where we lived as American missionaries. These two beautiful girls had left everything they knew behind: a crowded orphanage, rice fields, the dirty streets of Phnom Penh, even siblings. But their fear of the unknown was soon overpowered by their bright future.

We had hoped and prayed that their fear of hunger and abandonment eventually would be replaced by trust and love. Yet little did my husband and I know how much these two girls would change our lives also.

Sivy was thirteen when we met her, the youngest of four children in a family left orphaned and devastated by AIDS. She was born in a small, rural village in the Svay Rieng Province of southeast Cambodia. Her family farmed several small plots of land and grew rice for a living.

Like many poor Cambodian children, Sivy began working in the rice fields at age eight. She also tended the family cow and nursed her mother, who had contracted AIDS from her father after he returned from a civil war that defeated the Khmer Rouge.

Sivy's father died when she was eight years old. Her mother died two years later. By age ten, Sivy had known more grief and loss than any little girl should. Left in the care of the village, she and her sisters sang at the Buddhist temple and attended school sporadically.

Not long after both her parents died, her uncle placed her in an orphanage in Phnom Penh. Sivy was ten-and-a-half the day she was taken there, and she was not happy about the decision.

Sopheak was nine when we met her. She was born in an area of Phnom Penh known as "The Dump." It had no running water, no toilets, no electricity, and no paved streets. The occupants collected garbage off the streets of Phnom Penh at night and then hauled it back to the dump in push carts.

Sopheak frequently accompanied family members through the dark streets of the crowded city and played—without toys—in the dump. She was passed around, from her biological mother to later stepmothers, until her uncle took her at age five, with her sister, to the orphanage. He promised them many pretty dresses and a swimming pool in their new home. And she believed him. But she never saw pretty dresses or a swimming pool. As days plunged into weeks and months, the harsh reality of conditions at the orphanage frequently brought her to tears.

My husband, Paul, was fifty-seven, and I was two weeks shy of fifty-four, on the Christmas night when the girls arrived. We had no idea how rough our road would be for the next four years as we fought to make these girls legally our own. But we did have clear direction from the Lord when we said "yes" to taking the girls from the orphanage. Not long after, we realized we had not stopped to ask a few obvious questions:

Are these two little girls emotionally healthy? Can we legally adopt them? Will they ever be allowed to travel to the USA with us? How will we communicate, since they speak only Khmer? Will they even want to stay with us?

We knew God wanted these girls to have an opportunity to go to school, to have a family and a clean place to call home. Our hearts were bigger than our wallets, though we did have plenty of love and experience with children. So, convinced that God had led us to these girls, we were willing to follow Him one day at a time. And each day, for months to come, brought new adventures, filled with growth and miracles.

Chapter 2

Timely Detour

PAUL AND I grew up in solid families. Our happy childhoods and middle-class working values molded us into confident young adults. But in those days, neither of us truly sought the Lord's direction. We fell in love and were married in 1972, while I was in college finishing a degree in special education and he was teaching junior high. After six happy years of marriage, we had three little boys and two master's degrees. We lived in the suburbs, drove a station wagon, and dreamed of someday owning a summer cabin.

Fourteen years later, we both taught school and still drove the station wagon. The boys were all healthy, and we lived a typical American family's life in the Chicago suburbs. By this time, we attended church and prayed for wisdom to raise our boys. Our dream of a summer cabin came a bit closer to reality when we purchased a piece of lakefront property. Foreign lands and adopted children were nowhere in our thoughts or prayers.

Then, in October of 1986, while I was at a convention for Christian teachers, I picked up a brochure on teaching overseas. It invited teachers to serve in Papua New Guinea (PNG), teaching missionary children.

This was a new concept to me; I really knew nothing about missions. So I brought the brochure home and showed it to Paul.

"Where is Papua New Guinea?" he asked.

We found it on a map and briefly discussed the job request. But the whole idea was far beyond our conception of reality, considering we had three boys, a house payment, seven hundred dollars in the savings account, and a now-junky station wagon!

And though we each tried to get the idea out of our minds, God had planted a seed in our hearts. So we mailed in the response card and inquired further about the teaching positions in PNG. God went before us to open doors. Barely seven months after I picked up the brochure, we were on our way to Papua New Guinea. God had led us to the other side of the world, to a land of the unexpected.

Our passports were sent to the PNG Embassy in Washington, DC, so we could get the correct visa to enter this faraway country. However, the passports got lost somewhere in the embassy. We already had purchased five cheap, no-changes-allowed, non-refundable tickets, but we could not leave without passports and visas.

Everyone we knew was praying for our passports to be found before the date of departure. However, they were not found in time. So airline personnel rewrote our plane tickets to read, "Depart Chicago, arrive Honolulu," and "Depart Honolulu, arrive Papua New Guinea." That way, we could leave on time and wait in Hawaii for the passports to be found and airmailed to us there.

This was our first experience in waiting on God's timing—a lesson we would re-learn over and over again throughout our lives as missionaries. Yes, God wanted us in PNG, but first he had an important person for us to meet in Hawaii.

As we waited for our documents, Paul built cabinets for a mission organization in exchange for housing for our family. Tom Patrick was the head of the building team, and he and Paul became good friends. Our boys and I enjoyed discovering all the free events on the island and swimming at the beach while Paul worked.

After three weeks, the passports arrived. We said our good-byes and left three weeks behind schedule, totally unaware that our new relationship with Tom Patrick would resurface eighteen years later, in an amazing way—via Cambodia.

After one year of daily life in Papua New Guinea and teaching missionary kids, our family was positively changed forever. So we returned to the States, sold everything, completed more missionary training, and returned to PNG in 1990, now as career missionaries. We built a house there and raised our sons in the mountains. It was our home, and we thought we would be there until we retired. However, God again had a different plan.

When our youngest son, Nathan, finished high school, it was 1997 and time to travel back to the States and get him settled in college. It was also our twenty-fifth wedding anniversary. So in celebration, we planned a trip through Europe on our way back to PNG.

The last stop on our trip home was Chiang Mai, Thailand. There we visited friends and a small mission school. During that visit, our missionary friends challenged us to join a start-up team for a new international school. It was planned to serve many different mission organizations, while also reaching out to the Thai community. We were excited about the prospect and felt that God was behind the project.

So in December, 1997, we changed plans and moved to Thailand as "empty nesters." And in August, 1999, Grace International School officially opened. Paul and I both took teaching positions. Life was good, and so were our plans. We would teach in Thailand and enjoy quiet vacations—just the two of us—in the tropics. And that's exactly what we did for the next five years. But once again, God had a different plan.

Chapter 3

The One in Pink

OCTOBER 31, 2004, is a date etched in our hearts forever. On that day, while still in Chiang Mai, Paul and I enjoyed a meal after church at the Sizzler® in the Central Mall. The restaurant was crowded, so our table was moved right up against the large window that overlooked the entrance to the mall. But Paul didn't want that table. And though he said it felt like sitting in a fish bowl, we decided to stay anyway. As we ate, we clearly saw everyone entering the mall.

Then suddenly, Paul startled me. "That man in the khaki hat looks familiar," he said.

We exchanged glances through the window. And before we could get up, the man in the khaki hat entered the restaurant and stood at our table. It was Tom Patrick, the same man we'd said "good-bye" to in Hawaii eighteen years earlier!

He was as surprised as we were and explained he had finished his nursing degree and was now leading medical teams throughout South East Asia. He had most recently left Cambodia, where he'd worked with an orphanage. Of course, we invited him to tour Grace International School, and he accepted.

The next day, Tom came to visit our ministries at Grace, and Paul was excited to show him what the Lord had done there. Later in the day, the three of us sat in my second-grade classroom after school and talked about the Lord's goodness.

Tom told us more about his medical work in the orphanage in Phnom Penh, Cambodia, and how a bright little girl named Sopheak had captured his heart there. He believed God had great things in store for her life. "Ever since I left Cambodia, I've been praying for God to send the right couple to adopt Sopheak," he told us with conviction.

Paul and I were moved by his concern. We immediately made a list of all the couples we thought would be good adoptive parents.

"No, don't make a list," Tom said. "I am asking you two to adopt Sopheak."

I cut a look at Paul, needing to see his first reaction. But you can imagine the thoughts that flew through my mind as we sat there—unable to speak, but thinking:

This cannot be happening!
I'm too old.
I'm so comfortable.
I'm busy at school.
Why would God ask me?

Paul and I finally recovered enough to shake our heads decisively and say, "No. That's impossible. We could not adopt a nine-year-old!"

Undeterred, Tom asked us to pray about it, and we agreed. We are missionaries. Of course, we had to agree to pray!

So I earnestly prayed for a good home for Sopheak. God could certainly find her a good home—one that would not include me.

Tom left the next day for the States. And less than a week later, he attached this exact picture in an email that read simply: "She is the one in pink" (middle).

Now I had a face crowding into my prayers, and suddenly those prayers intensified. Soon after, when Paul went away for a weekend event, I decided to pray and fast. We had not told anyone about our visit with Tom or about his request. First we had prayed together for direction; now we prayed separately.

A dear friend stopped by that same weekend to give me a book. We often shared books, and I welcomed her gift. She did not know I was fasting, nor did she know anything about Sopheak. The book *A Hunger for God* by John Piper was about prayer and fasting, and I knew God was moving in my heart, so I started reading it right away. One scripture passage in that book is quoted from Isaiah:

> Is not this the kind of fasting I have chosen: to loose the chains of injustice and untie the cords of the yoke, to set the oppressed free and

> break every yoke? Is it not to share your food with the hungry and to provide the poor wanderer with shelter—when you see the naked, to clothe him, and not to turn away from your own flesh and blood?
>
> —Isaiah 58:6–7

As I read the words, I knew God was speaking directly to me and answering my prayers about a home for Sopheak—and I wept. How could God choose me, at age fifty-four, to mother a nine-year-old from Cambodia?

When Paul returned from his trip, with obvious reluctance, he asked, "What did God tell you?"

I was afraid to answer him. I knew God would not tell each of us anything contradictory, but I wanted him to answer first, so I sidestepped his question. "What did God tell you?"

Paul drew a deep breath and looked me straight in the eyes. "I think God is asking us to go to Cambodia. I'm not sure about taking a child, but I think we met Tom for a reason."

Paul's answer confirmed what God had told me.

Chapter 4

Piece by Piece

BEFORE WE COULD purchase tickets to Cambodia, we had to talk to the school administration at Grace International School (GIS). Paul and I both had signed teaching contracts, with responsibilities to match.

Plus, bringing a child into our home presented another problem. All new students have to pass an English Proficiency test before they can enroll at GIS, because classes are taught in English. But Sopheak could not speak any English, and my teaching assignment would prevent me from homeschooling her. So this puzzle began to reveal many new pieces, and only God had the foreknowledge to put them together.

Paul covered me in prayer the day I went to speak with the elementary school principal. Her decision could close the door on the adoption idea, at least until the end of the school year. I thought perhaps I could be released from my teaching position. But I did not want that to happen either. Maybe Sopheak could be admitted to school as an exception, even without any English proficiency. But then, how would she learn?

I explained to the principal how we'd met Tom Patrick. I told her about God's direction and how we thought this discussion might be the end of our journey to Cambodia.

Then she turned to me and spoke kindly. "Paula, if God is leading you to take this child, who am I to stand in the way? I'll go to the Board and back you in this. I trust your professional decision to bring back a child who will learn quickly and thrive academically at GIS. But she will have to maintain passing grades, to keep a student visa."

Her gracious response left me stunned! The pieces of our puzzle were fitting together instead of falling apart. But I was still not sure we could be Sopheak's parents. Maybe God was using us to bring her to Thailand, only to be adopted by someone else. At this point, I could only pray, "Lord, help me be obedient. Make your way clear to me."

With barely-controlled excitement, we contacted Tom Patrick and shared our decision to go to Cambodia to meet Sopheak. A missionary he knew, Martin, worked at the Phnom Penh orphanage and also knew Sopheak. So we emailed Martin our itinerary and told him our school could provide a student visa for Sopheak to study in Thailand and live with us.

At this point, we had not yet even met Sopheak, let alone gotten her opinion on the idea. But she was still "the one in pink," who consumed my daily thoughts and prayers.

We hadn't considered the legal processes needed to take a minor across the border from Cambodia to Thailand. All we really knew was that we were going to Cambodia to meet a little girl who needed an opportunity. She needed an education to open up the world. And most of all, that tiny girl in pink needed a loving family to fill her life. As I packed my suitcase, I prayed, "Please make your will clear to us, Lord. Are we to raise this little girl?"

Chapter 5

Arrival in Cambodia

MARTIN MET US at the airport in Phnom Penh. A Norwegian, he was much younger than we'd imagined him to be. But he was fluent in English and Khmer, and we liked him right away.

Martin worked in the streets of the city, ministering to the poor. He also helped with the children at the orphanage where Sopheak lived. He was excited that Paul and I had come and shared stories about what a sweet girl she was. But we were tired from travel, and the hour was late, so we drove straight to our hotel that night.

As a missionary, I have lived in a lot of places. I've driven through the indescribably wild traffic of Bangkok, Manila, and Manaus. But *nothing* could have prepared me for the chaos of the streets of Phnom Penh.

We dodged motorcycles and ox-driven carts coming toward us from all directions. There simply were *no* rules. Traffic lights cycled regularly from red to green, but they seemed to make little difference to the drivers. And though the month was December, hot dust filled my nostrils as a cacophony of horns assaulted my ears.

We arrived at a large, locally-run hotel that provided our basic needs. The sheets were clean, though they had holes. There was a shower, but no curtain to keep water within the proper area. So we reminded ourselves that this was not a luxury trip. It was just uncomfortable enough to keep the realities of a wild city on my mind.

On the other side of our wall lived many beggars. Families slept on the streets and in crowded alleyways. Hungry, scantily-clothed children and starving dogs seemed to be everywhere. I tried to sleep, but street images from the past two hours since my arrival in Phnom Penh haunted me. Young men had missing limbs as a result of Khmer Rouge landmines. Toothless women's mouths dripped the blood-red juice of betel nuts. Small children sniffed glue outside our window as we ate dinner.

I eventually accepted the fact that our uncomfortable bed had a great purpose. It kept me awake to pray. And I repeatedly told myself that tomorrow morning I would meet Sopheak. Unbelievably, only thirty-five days had passed since my husband and I first heard about her. This merry-go-round was spinning fast, but we kept our balance in the middle of it.

At 7 A.M. the next morning, I waited in the hotel lobby, enjoying a little "quiet" time with my Bible and a free cup of coffee. But the lobby was anything but quiet.

Dozens of beautiful Cambodian girls walked in and out, heavily made-up, dressed in short, tight skirts. Some left with foreign men; others scurried out alone, making no eye contact with anyone. I was obviously in the company of prostituted women—but women whom God loved. As I sat, I wondered if they ever had heard the name of Jesus.

I knew my God was bigger than the noise around me that morning, and when I called upon Him, He was there. I reread the Scripture verses that had so clearly led us thus far on our journey.

> Is not this the kind of fasting I have chosen: to loose the chains of injustice and untie the cords of the yoke, to set the oppressed free and break every yoke? Is it not to share your food with the hungry and

to provide the poor wanderer with shelter—when you see the naked,
to clothe him, and not to turn away from your own flesh and blood?
—Isaiah 58:6–7

Martin joined us after breakfast, and we rode in a two-seated tuk-tuk to the orphanage. Even with my overseas experiences, what I experienced this particular morning was beyond anything I could have imagined. We were in the midst of a dirty, crowded city, with traffic screeching around us in all directions. New smells and noises engulfed me. We passed filthy young children—four or five years old—wandering the streets, totally alone. Their large, brown eyes and outstretched hands brought me to tears.

As we bumped along a littered dirt road, behind a fence of scrap wood and concrete, children ran to open a metal gate, and then we entered a dirt yard. The orphanage was a small, single-story building, without window screens.

Two girls washed their clothes in a large, plastic tub and hung them on a makeshift clothesline strung along the side of the fence. A small guard shack leaned against the front gate, where a withered old man stoked his small fire. The children wore smiles instead of shoes and played happily with nothing but each other. As much as the conditions of the physical building depressed me, their smiles and laughter were encouraging.

One staff worker and the director welcomed us as we entered the main room of the orphanage. The floor was concrete. And because of a large, open gap between the walls and the corrugated-metal roof, the structure provided no protection from the hard tropical rains or swarms of insects. Three computers sat on old, wooden tables; one was turned on. Faded instructional posters were miraculously mounted on the dirty, water-stained, concrete walls. Piles of cardboard boxes littered the corners.

Paul and I sat at a low table with Martin, surrounded by the director, an interpreter, and a teacher. They told us the orphanage was built four years ago. It housed eighteen girls and twenty-nine boys. It was operated by a local non-government organization (NGO) and supported by donations from numerous groups, representing several countries. Most importantly, they explained the site had paperwork on each child, giving the orphanage legal custody over them.

These employees liked our idea of providing a scholarship for one of the orphans to study at Grace International School. We spent about an hour and a half together, looking at the GIS yearbooks that we had brought. We shared a bit about our family and teaching experiences.

The director told us about the food, shelter, and opportunities his NGO provided for the needy children. Then we took a tour of the facilities and saw the orphans' primitive living conditions.

All eighteen girls shared one small room. There was one bed made of wooden planks. It had no mattress. In the corner, open-sided boxes were stacked almost to the ceiling, serving as dressers, and several little shirts hung on hangers over the few nails that were able to stay in the walls.

The bathroom was adjacent the girls' room. This "toilet" consisted of a simple hole in the floor that was surrounded by tile. A large, clay pot filled with water and a ladle stood next to the hole, and the girls used it both to flush and to wash. The stench instantly nauseated me, but I forced myself to smile as I greeted a barefoot teenage girl in a school uniform. Her job was to clean the walls and floor by splashing water on them. That's all that was available.

We passed through a little hallway that served as the kitchen. It consisted of a concrete sink that was placed within a low counter approximately four feet long. Two coal fires burned on one end of the counter; one fire had a large, black pot on it. This room was also where girls washed their dishes on the concrete floor, using merely a hose and a large, plastic tub.

The boys slept outside on wooden "beds," also without mattresses, though several beds were broken. Martin recently had bought mosquito nets to protect the boys at night. The kids both ate and played on wooden tables and benches on the back porch.

Beyond the kitchen porch, three makeshift classrooms contained more wooden tables, benches, and a white board—but no walls. I had trouble comprehending how forty-seven children lived in two rooms and a covered porch area. No one had a space of his or her own.

Most of the children were at the nearest public school when we arrived at the orphanage. The young ones attended classes in the morning, and the older ones studied in the afternoon. But the children who were present greeted us warmly and immediately brought us their English notebooks. The littlest ones crawled on my lap and simply wanted a hug. I encouraged their English and hugged them, while I waited for Sopheak to return from school.

Chapter 6

Double Blessing

I RECOGNIZED SOPHEAK immediately, from the picture that Tom Patrick had sent. She sparkled as she entered with all her little friends. Her smile was brilliant, and she seemed to be the leader of the group. All the kids were eager to greet me, although none of them knew why we were there. All they knew was that visitors often brought gifts, and so the children clamored around.

Here I was, face-to-face with the small nine-year-old girl who had consumed my thoughts, dreams, and prayers during the past month. Sopheak wore her public school uniform. She looked clean and cared for. But she was so tiny that I would have guessed her to be only seven, instead of nine years old, if I hadn't seen all the permanent teeth in her smile. Her hair was short, irregularly cut—and full of lice. She proudly greeted me with the few English phrases she had memorized.

"Hello."

"How are you?"

"Fine, thank you. And you?"

A bit later, when she ran into the girls' room to change into play clothes, my prayer was surprisingly clear. "Please, Lord, let me be the one to mother this child."

Once I saw Sopheak, I was ashamed to think that I ever had wanted to say "no." My reasons had been so selfish. Now I called on the Lord for strength and wisdom to obey. The task of raising another child was huge, especially at my age, but I could not see myself doing anything else. I loved her already.

Sopheak let me comb her hair, clearly enjoying the attention. I gave her the comb when I was done, and she was thrilled. It was hers! The children at the orphanage did not have many personal items. They shared a comb that was tied to a string and nailed to a wooden pole. Her gratitude for such a simple thing humbled me.

Sopheak and I worked together with paper and a pencil. She drew detailed pictures that indicated great creativity, imagination, and fine motor skills. The picture she drew of me resembled a queen in a long gown. She could copy letters of the English alphabet and write her name in both Khmer and English.

She quickly learned to play tic-tac-toe and the dot game. We communicated through pictures and hand motions, and she quickly played the games competitively. She was bright and animated in everything she tried. Drawing on my twenty-five years of teaching experience, I felt confident that she could learn English and succeed at Grace.

Then, to our surprise, Martin and the director of the orphanage encouraged us to take *two* children! They said that the adjustment of moving to a new country, living in a Western-style home, and starting a new school in a foreign language would be traumatic for Sopheak. However, a peer whom she knew and could communicate with might reduce that stress.

Their rationale made sense, but I was not prepared to take two children. *God, is this coming from you? Are we supposed to take two children?* I thought.

Paul and I went back to the hotel that night and prayed intensely. Again, the uncomfortable bed kept me up most of the night. And again, I asked God to give us clear direction.

"What are we to do? And if we take a second child, how will we choose one from the forty-seven children living in the orphanage? Should we choose a boy or a girl, and what age?"

When we'd started this journey to Cambodia, we were not positive we'd even take one child, and now I sensed God asking me to take two!

After worshipping in a local Khmer church the next morning, we headed back to the orphanage with Martin. When we arrived, the children were watching their weekly video. The crowded, dirty conditions of the room were depressing, and I found myself longing to find homes for every one of those precious little ones. Their situation seemed so unfair. Why couldn't we take them all? But I knew that was impossible. The reality of orphanage life left me thinking wild thoughts.

Paul, Martin, and I joined the orphanage director and a staff member at a low table covered with a stained cloth. The staff member, who spoke limited English, tried to explain some paperwork to me. I soon understood that he was showing me three report cards. He had chosen three children whom he thought should go to Grace to study—but Sopheak was not one of them!

We explained to Martin that if we took any child, it would be Sopheak; she was the one whom God had chosen for us. Martin explained our feelings to the staff in Khmer. Sopheak was the child we came for, but we would listen and consider their recommendations for a second child.

The main focus of the conversation was the grades on the report cards. Everyone was talking quickly in Khmer. And they all seemed to agree on something that I did not understand. In my frustration, I jumped in and picked up a random report card and waved it in the air.

"Whose report card is this?"

"Sivy's," Martin said.

"Where is she?" I asked.

"In the kitchen."

I immediately went to find her. When I saw her standing by the concrete counter, I remembered her from the day before. She had not been one of the children who had pushed their way to the front to get my attention.

I started to talk to Sivy, and much to my surprise, she responded in clear but limited English. She was quick to ask me to repeat something if she did not understand. She smiled sincerely and quickly looked back at her work.

"What are you doing?" I asked.

"I am cutting," she said.

"What are you cutting?"

She paused, then answered confidently with a broad smile, "I do not know in English."

"It looks like a carrot," I said, "except it is white."

"Then I will call it a white carrot!"

We both laughed. Sivy was a bright child.

As she finished cutting the white carrot, she used hand motions and her limited English to tell me that she was thirteen years old and the youngest of four siblings. Martin already had told me that her parents had died of AIDS, her siblings were scattered, and Sivy had lived with her grandmother in a rural village near the Vietnam border.

Sivy had worked in the rice fields, cared for her grandmother, and gone to school sporadically. She had developed a chronic skin disease on her knee, which required medical attention that she couldn't get in the village. Ultimately, because of the chronic skin disease, Sivy was sent to this orphanage in the city.

Sivy knew why we were there, since the director had told the older children that we would choose two of them to study in Thailand. I wondered what was going through her mind as I talked with her.

When it was time for the orphanage's weekly worship service, Sivy gathered all the little children and sat them on the front bench. Then she gathered the older children and helped them all to find a seat.

One of the staff members played the guitar, and Sivy led the children in song. She used hand motions to express the meaning of the words. The little ones followed her. When the music was finished, she quietly took a seat in the back and listened intently to the message.

Paul and I worshipped with the children. And when the last songs were sung, I knew whom God had chosen as the second child. We met with the director after the worship service to continue our discussion about taking a second child. We did not know it at the time, but Sivy had overheard part of that conversation. She *thought* she heard Paul say, "No. Sivy is too old."

And though Sivy never had prayed much before, at that moment, she ran to the girls' room, threw herself onto the wooden bed, and cried out to the Lord. Her heart was broken to be considered and rejected. She was so in agony, she prayed aloud for the first time. "Jesus, let me be the one to go."

And with that simple cry for help, she believed.

Paul and I had no idea at the time that the Lord was working so mightily in her heart, but it was clear to us that He had chosen for us to raise Sopheak and Sivy. God had doubled the blessing!

Chapter 7

The Girls Remember

IN SOPHEAK'S WORDS:

The orphanage was small, and it was near a busy street. We slept on wooden planks. I did not know the difference between comfortable and uncomfortable back then, so it did not matter. I had heard about beds but had never seen one. We ate on tin plates. Our Cambodian food was rice, rice porridge, soy sauce, fish, and soup with a lot of green vegetables. We did not have a lot of food, but we did eat three times a day. Noodles were a special treat that we rarely got. It was my favorite.

Every morning we had to wake up at four o'clock and do exercises for an hour. Sometimes I would pretend to be sick so I would not have to get up and exercise, but it did not quite work. Then after the exercises, we cleaned the orphanage.

Once, my best friend stole a lot of money from the other kids in the orphanage. She told me that if I promised not to tell anyone, she would buy me something. I knew where she hid the money. The kids were wondering where their money was, and I told the director and everybody. I do not remember my friend getting mad at me or being punished, but I do remember telling the truth.

One day, a team of medical missionaries came to help, and this is how the story of my second chance started. The story is so exciting!

Most of the time, I had pink eye, which is a disease that made my eyelids stick together when I woke up. When I peeled open my eyes, it hurt. One of the men from the medical team came to help me. His name was Tom Patrick, but I called him Papa Tom. He was one of the first foreigners I met. He was gentle and looked trustworthy. He had a short beard, soft hair, blue eyes, and red cheeks.

He asked me a question in English, but I did not understand, so I called out to the translator. He had asked if he could help me with my eyes. I said, "Yes" in Khmer. The translator told Papa Tom everything I said. The missionaries brought us toothpaste and brushes. They boiled our mosquito nets and taught us how to wash our hands.

One night, Papa Tom brought me a basket of fruit, but the orphanage took it. I don't think Papa Tom knew. He rocked me in a chair and sang me a song. I didn't understand the English, but the tune and the words made me feel special. The next morning, I asked where Papa Tom was. I found out he was gone. I ran to the girls' room and cried.

After Papa Tom left, I did not know where he was or what he was doing, but God knew. God told Papa Tom to find a family for me. I did not know it, but he went to Chiang Mai, Thailand. While he was there, he went to Sizzler®, and there in the window he noticed two very old friends, Paul and Paula Jarot, whom he had not seen for eighteen years. He was surprised to see them. Papa Tom spent the next day with these friends and believed that they were the family God had for me.

At first the Jarots said, "No, we are too old; but we will pray for a family for her." The more they prayed, the more they realized that God wanted them to take me as their daughter.

In Sivy's words:

When I first heard the plan to put me in the orphanage, I expected to receive lots of things according to my selfish desires. After my parents died in 2002, I was sent to a small orphanage in Phnom Penh, the capital city of Cambodia. I had so many expectations of this place. I thought living there would save me lots of money. I thought I would have nice clothes, delicious food, and my own room. But when I got there, I had no desire to stay.

The orphanage was nothing like what I dreamed of. It was small and needed so many provisions. I did not have my own room. In fact, a room for one person did not exist in the orphanage.

This small, rented shelter known as an 'orphanage' had only one bedroom, a small office, and a tiny kitchen. During my first night there, everyone in the orphanage, girls and boys and even the staff, slept on the concrete floor in the bedroom and office.

For each meal, the orphans could eat as much rice as they wanted, but they didn't have much cooked meat to eat with it. They did not abuse the orphans, but they did not have much to offer the hungry children.

The staff tried their best to find supporters. The children understood how severe the town's poverty was. Many orphans were grateful to be in that place because it was so much better than the place they came from.

All of us were hungry all the time. Teenage orphans like me usually went out to the rice field to collect green vegetables and snails for dinner. Some orphans, including me, tried to save some money to buy cooked chicken blood or hard-boiled, bad eggs for our special treat.

Each orphan worked hard every day. It wasn't so hard as to be abused, but we had many chores and responsibilities. I did not like living there. I tried to run away several times, but I never succeeded.

One day, I made it to my older sister's rented room to visit and begged to live with her. She lived in Phnom Penh and worked at a garment factory. I did not return to the orphanage on the day I was supposed to; and later, my sister tricked me into returning. I thought I was going to get my clothes and move in with her, but when I got to the orphanage, they made me stay.

Chapter 8

Sovereign Timing

AFTER MUCH PRAYER, Paul and I decided to take both girls home to Chiang Mai. So Sopheak and Sivy were issued an official letter of invitation to study at Grace International School. We worked with Martin to create a document that would allow the girls to live with us in Thailand.

Martin typed two documents, one in English and one in Khmer. They stated that Paul and I would take all responsibility for the care of the girls. We would provide housing, food, and medical care, but Mr. Meas, the director of the orphanage, maintained legal guardianship. We were only granted temporary guardianship so the girls could go to school.

The director showed us paperwork that legally declared both girls orphans. We also agreed in writing to communicate with the director and send back report cards and pictures. The document stated that Paul and I had legal authority to make decisions for the girls. It was notarized and signed by the director, Paul, and me. The girls had to apply for passports, so we also left money to cover that expense.

We made all these decisions so fast, and our lives have never been the same. I weighed the decision, placing opportunities and education for two orphaned girls on one side. On the other, I had viewed my comfort and busy schedule. Now, though I knew we made the right choice, the reality was hard to comprehend.

We had not researched the possibility of adopting the girls, but in the back of our minds, we certainly were taking them with that possible future intention. When we called our married sons in the United States, we announced their two new little sisters.

Sopheak had an older biological sister named Somphor, age fifteen, who lived at the orphanage and could not come to Thailand to stay, but we included her in the first trip to visit so that she could see the school and her sister's new home. Somphor agreed that the separation was worth the opportunity. Then before Sopheak left Cambodia, Martin took her and her sister back to the dump where they were raised, so they could talk to their aunt and get her "blessing" on the move.

Sivy also went back to her village to say "good-bye" to her grandmother, sisters, and brother. Her sister told her to be cautious, because she had heard that many Cambodian girls were being trafficked to Thailand. In her child-like faith, Sivy answered that she wanted to go and that it was right. She did not know Paul or me, but she trusted Martin.

Paul and I were thrown into an accelerated course, encompassing cross-cultural relations, international adoption, raising adolescents, and surviving mid-life crisis. Our vacation plans for a quiet Christmas on the beach in Thailand were quickly cancelled because the girls were scheduled to arrive in Chiang Mai on Christmas Day.

Our son Nathan and his wife, Lisa, flew over to help us and to meet their new sisters. Nathan and Lisa were calm, compassionate, and nurturing, and that was just what Paul and I needed. We bought a few last-minute essentials for the girls, like a rice cooker and lots of fresh fruit. We had a quiet Christmas dinner as the "former" Jarot family, and then we drove to the airport.

As we waited and waited and waited for the girls' plane, my excitement made the time slow to a snail's pace. I was anxious, and I did not know what to expect. But I knew that as soon as they arrived, my life would never be the same.

Sopheak and Sivy arrived at 8 P.M., with smiles and hugs. Martin and a staff member from the orphanage had accompanied them, along with Sopheak's sister Somphor. All the girls' worldly possessions fit into one small carry-on bag. We piled into a van and headed toward home. The girls stayed with us, and the young men stayed in a hotel in town.

Sopheak had arrived in Thailand wearing a pair of shoes that were about three sizes too big. Martin explained that she did not have her own shoes and that these were borrowed for the special trip. But they needed to be returned.

Sivy's shoes did fit her, but they also were borrowed. And Martin needed to take both pairs back to the orphanage for other children when he returned. Shoes for all three girls, including Somphor, became first on my shopping list.

When we arrived at our home, the girls had a barrage of new experiences. They never had been in a Western home with furniture, polished floors, and curtains. As simple as it was, it was a palace to the girls. They had their first bed with sheets, their first dolls, their first flushing toilet, and first shower. Sopheak enjoyed flushing and waving good-bye to the tissue, as it mysteriously disappeared down the drain! They bounced on the bed and giggled.

All three girls' hair was full of lice, and Sivy's hair was so long, it almost reached her waist. I asked Martin if I would hurt their feelings by giving lice shampoo treatments this soon after they'd arrived.

"They would love to be rid of the lice. It will be a real treat," he said.

So my daughter-in-law Lisa and I taught the girls to wash their hair three times with lice treatment shampoo. And instead of it being a chore, they laughed and enjoyed their first showers. Then they each dressed in pretty, new pajamas and came downstairs, where we combed the dead lice and nits away.

Later, after being with us for several years, Sivy recalled the scene: "It was twelve o'clock at night, and all of us were still sitting around combing our hair and picking out lice! I had never stayed up that late before. I couldn't speak English, but I could tell time. I thought foreigners didn't sleep at night!"

At long last, all three girls were tucked into one queen-sized bed for the night. I had taught my first English lesson without words—in the bathroom. The objective was to communicate love and acceptance. And our common denominator was a disdain for lice!

When we awakened the next morning, we received an urgent phone call from friends in the States, who wanted to know if we were all right. These friends did not know about the girls coming, and I did not understand the fear in their voices. Then they asked whether or not we had seen the news.

Paul turned on the TV, and we watched the coverage of the destruction the Asian tsunami had brought. The entire Phi Phi Island of Thailand was gone! The hotel where we had planned to spend Christmas was washed totally out to sea. The beaches of Thailand were demolished; thousands had lost their lives in a mere ten hours since our girls had arrived. We had planned a vacation on that exact beach—but God's direction to Cambodia had saved our lives.

Chapter 9

So Many Firsts

YEARS AFTER WE finished raising our first three children, our home was full of children's laughter again. Sopheak frequently delighted us with her spontaneous, animated personality. She communicated well with her hands and her eyes, and she repeated everything I said. Her favorite expressions were, "Very Good!" with two thumbs up, and, "No problem." Her first original sentence was, "I am hungry."

She thanked us for everything and expressed gratitude with folded hands and a little bow. When she passed gas, she grinned and immediately said, "Not me." Sopheak ate anything we gave her—and she ate a lot! Her favorite food was packaged noodles with hot spices. She loved her hair clips and hair bands, often wearing many at the same time. Sopheak seldom sat still, unless she was involved in a game or a puzzle. Very observant, her eyes sparkled with excitement over the simplest things.

After four days of living with us, Sopheak exhibited many positive changes. She understood more words each day and started to express herself in English. She was comfortable with "Daddy" and reached out to touch him. She made her bear Bala talk and expected us to talk back. She chose *Curious George* every time I asked her to get a book.

She caused us all to laugh, and we were overjoyed. She drew a picture in her journal of Mommy, Sopheak, and Daddy tucked in bed, with our shoes lined-up at the foot of the bed.

Sivy, on the other hand, embodied all the sweetness of innocence and the strength of independence. Her simple, rural life and the poverty that had forced her to work in the fields, plus her mother's illness and death and the responsibility of caring for an elderly grandmother, had all molded Sivy into a beautiful, confident, capable young girl. She smiled from deep within, and her quick giggle and modesty were refreshing.

She was feminine, loving having her hair combed and trying on pretty dresses. She was a joy to watch, twirling in front of a full-length mirror. She had a tender spirit, and this showed when she brought me the pictures of her mother, father, grandmother, and siblings. She was a little mother to Sopheak, determined to do everything perfectly right in their new home.

Sivy expressed gratitude openly, but she was guarded when it came to expressing any negative emotion. She would not share her trials or tears of adjustment with us. I prayed that, over time, we could build a relationship on trust, one with a foundation of unconditional love.

She carried a Khmer/English dictionary with her everywhere. Sivy would search for a word in Khmer, and I would read its meaning in English. This way, I helped her build simple sentences around a topic that she was trying to communicate. She also used her dictionary to help me understand what Sopheak was trying to say.

We spent hours with English picture dictionaries and children's books. I purposely limited videos to one each week. Our girls did not know enough English to understand the theme of the movies, and they needed much practice repeating the new words they were exposed to.

Both girls were like intellectual sponges. Every day they surprised us with their new language ability. Sivy thought everything through before she spoke and analyzed all her sentences. But Sopheak simply talked and talked and talked!

After the girls were with us one week, we went to the doctor. I chose a female pediatrician for their first visit. Sivy was too old to go to a pediatrician, but I wanted a doctor who could catch them up on their immunizations. I also wanted both girls to go to the same doctor.

We had a long visit in the waiting room, but it was a good opportunity to work on our English. Sopheak rode on a little toy zebra made of metal, which glided back and forth. She was fascinated by the baby toys and played with the beads that travel along curved, metal poles and a little turtle that bobbed its head as you pushed it on the floor. She was nine years old and playing with baby toys for the first time. If there was something new to explore, she was eager to try.

As I told Sopheak's story to the doctor, she was amazed but not unaware of such circumstances. She was gentle and kind, and Sopheak went willingly to her. The doctor examined Sopheak and concluded that she was healthy; there were no signs of malnutrition or anemia. She weighed 23 kilograms (50 pounds), which is not much for a nine-year-old child.

She had her first immunizations, and we went to the hospital for chest x-rays. Whenever her charming personality popped out, the doctor laughed over and over again. Sopheak recognized a picture of Mickey Mouse on a calendar, but Sivy did not.

Sivy loved all the babies in the waiting room and greeted all the young mothers with a smile. And when it was her turn, she willingly went into the examining room, and I went with her. Everything went well, and she got the first of many immunizations. The disease on her knee was healed now but deeply scarred. Thankfully, the doctor explained that her knee was not internally damaged; Sivy would have full use of that knee and leg. She was very healthy and weighed 41 kilograms (90 pounds).

Sivy continued to use more English words every day. She worked so hard, trying to learn as much as she could before the first day of school. Soon she proudly announced, "I can understand two books," holding *From Head to Toe* and *Five Little Monkeys Jumping on the Bed.* She re-read them often and wrote Khmer language notes on the pages, to remember and understand all the words, sentence structures, and pictures.

After that accomplishment, I took her to my second-grade classroom to find more books to work on. I pulled out one book that began: "Once upon a time, there was a little house in the country."

She was frustrated with the phrase "Once upon a time" and wanted a literal translation. I tried to explain but failed.

"How can I go to grade six? I cannot read grade two," she cried in frustration.

My heart broke, seeing her trying hard and feeling so defeated. The task before her seemed impossible, yet she still progressed with confidence.

We bought Sopheak a twenty-inch bicycle with a basket and training wheels. She was nine years old but had never had the opportunity to learn to ride. For three days, she practiced riding her beautiful, new bike and soon got used to steering it. One time, she accidently ran into me and knocked me over into the field.

"Mommy, I'm sorry," she said over and over again.

I wasn't hurt, and we all laughed. But soon after that, she hit a parked truck. Days later, when she was balancing and steering much better, the training wheels came off. But she still couldn't ride far without falling over often—though that didn't slow her down much.

She said "bicycle" clearly now, and it was the first word out of her mouth in the mornings. She had one crash that brought tears, but she got back on the bike. I was thankful that my son Nate was visiting in Thailand, so he could run behind the bike for a while. But after he departed, Paul and I had to take turns—and I felt my age. It took several months of practice, until she finally could ride by herself.

Sivy chose a bright red bike with a basket and a rider's seat on the back fender. At the store, when we pushed it up to the checkout counter, she said over and over, "Is it mine? Do I get a new one?" She never had owned a bike and certainly had never even dreamed of having a new one.

My fifty-fourth birthday got lost in all the commotion of January 8, 2005. Paul forgot, and the girls did not know what birthdays were.

They only had been with us for two weeks, and I didn't care about a celebration or a gift because I was so grateful for this new opportunity to raise Sopheak and Sivy. God had given me two "Cambodian jewels."

By the second week in January, all our company had left, and the normal, everyday realities of our new family began. We wove English into every activity. Whether we were shopping, cooking, traveling, or relaxing at home, I taught English.

Sopheak thought it was a game to mimic everything I said. She quickly learned the phrase, "What is it?" and used it repeatedly. She continued to talk all the time, though with a limited vocabulary, but it grew each day. She loved to draw pictures, and we talked about her drawings. Soon, she was correcting me, if I didn't interpret her drawing precisely.

Christmas break was almost over, and we were preparing for the girls' first day of school. One event was a trip to the mall, to buy shoes to wear with their new dresses. The girls were overwhelmed with all the choices, so both girls simply chose the first pair they tried on. Sopheak even wore hers home, but Sivy did not. Sivy somehow understood that her gym shoes went with the casual outfit she wore, so she saved her new shoes for school and to wear with her pretty dress.

We had to return the swimsuits I had purchased before the girls arrived. They didn't like tank-style suits, saying they were "too revealing." The girls preferred swimsuits with little skirts. Every time Sopheak saw a two-piece swimsuit on display, she shook her finger and said, "No, no, no."

Sivy merely giggled. "I do not like this one. It is not good." So through my girls' eyes, I began to realize how different their culture was from mine, in almost every way.

Later, as we walked through rows of nightgowns, Sivy took one off the rack, held it up to me, and said, "Oh, pretty, Mommy." They both laughed—and Paul couldn't get out of the department fast enough.

For weeks, we found it interesting that each girl's limited language abilities in English did not hinder their different personalities from shining through. Sopheak was my princess. She was full of life, always ready for a party and ready to try anything. On the other hand, Sivy was strong and confident in a quiet and unassuming way. She was quick to smile, and it was clear her joy came from true gratitude.

Soon it was time for the first day of school. Sopheak faced the challenge like David standing before Goliath. On the first day, she was up early, dressed in her uniform, and sitting at the breakfast table with a big smile. She was in my own second-grade class, and I had told all the other children about her before they had left for Christmas break.

She was a novelty in our class and enjoyed being the center of attention. She also carefully observed and copied the other children's behavior. With the help of my student teacher, we kept constant communication with her by using simple words and hand motions.

Several times during the first month of school, she hit her frustration level. She tried so hard to keep up with the class and wanted her school papers to look like everyone else's. But her frustration sometimes led to tears and then to wails, until she had to be removed from the classroom. That's when I'd quickly carry her—screaming—into the nurse's office.

Our school nurse had worked with street kids in Venezuela, so she was familiar with kids who struggled with attachment disorders. She asked me to lie down beside Sopheak on the nurse room bed and simply let her cry. I held her, stroked her hair, and assured her that I was not leaving and that I loved her. This tiny nine-year-old eventually melted in my arms and hugged me tightly. When she was calm and ready, we went back to class as if nothing had happened.

Sopheak clearly remembers her first day of school:

> I was not afraid to go to school. I was not afraid of anything back then, not snakes or dogs or new people or anything. On the first day of school, I was up early, because I was used to getting up at 4:30 A.M. at the orphanage. I liked the hair clips and wore them all at once. Nothing matched, but I did not care. I would never do that

today. I did not think school was too hard; I just followed everyone. All the kids were nice to me, but I don't think I could go to a new school without speaking the language now. I was not afraid of anything then. Everything was an adventure.

Sivy also remembers her first day of school in Thailand, at thirteen years old. But I can't imagine myself doing what she did.

Have you ever been transferred to a new school? If you have, did you also have to learn a new language in order to function in that school?

Not too many students switch schools and languages at the same time. I am one of the few who have done so. And I tell you, it wasn't very enjoyable. Four years ago, I faced many unexpected difficulties, especially learning how to read a sixth-grade novel for homework, when I could hardly understand a first-grade reading book.

Having adoptive American parents wasn't the most troublesome adjustment, but learning to speak their language was quite challenging. It was one of the biggest changes in my life. It was a pleasurable change, though. Coming from a Cambodian orphanage, I had some hard times, trying to adjust my lifestyle to be more Westernized because of my Western parents.

The most difficult thing about living with my new parents was not being able to communicate or understand their conversations. Mommy taught me how to read every day. She took me to her second-grade class and found some easy books for me. Most of them were too hard for me to understand, but Mom did not give up on me. She tried to teach me how to read again and again. A few days after my first day of school at Grace International School (GIS), I read and understood the story *Five Little Monkeys Jumping on the Bed.* I was overjoyed, and I jumped on the bed myself!

I wondered, *Will I fit in at this new school?* The answer was, fit or not, I am going to GIS. And I am going to learn English!

Shifting from a little Khmer public school, I thought GIS wasn't the kind of school for me. It was too luxurious. It was the kind of

> school for wealthy, talented, beautiful, and intelligent students. They were the opposite of me.
>
> Sixth grade at GIS in 2005 was the hardest year of schooling in my life. I was nowhere near the top of the class. I was shy and embarrassed whenever the teacher asked me a question, because I didn't know the answers. And every time I spoke, all eyes were on me, due to my funny accent. People looked at me closely and watched my mouth so that they could have a better idea of what I was saying.
>
> Since I had little understanding of English, homework dominated my life after school. It took much time and effort to study, so I had less time to play. I spent five to six hours a day getting my homework finished. Sixth-grade homework wasn't difficult or time-consuming for English-speaking students, but it was extremely hard for me.
>
> I did not have time for after-school sports. I also could not attend the special Thai class like other students. At home, I cried—many times. Sometimes I cried with Mommy and sometimes by myself.

Sivy strove for excellence in everything she did, and she aimed to please, unlike many thirteen-year-olds. She was always smiling and liked physical touch. She wanted to hold my hand or Paul's wherever we walked. She read her Khmer Bible every night, after she climbed into bed. Her teachers praised her, and she applied her daily vocabulary lessons at school to her spoken English at home, often sounding many years older and quite scholarly, with sentences like: "The plane ride to America will be interminable." "My sister exasperates me!" "I am apprehensive about my science test on Friday." "I learned to speak distinctly."

She amazed everyone who met her. She was and is brilliant. She crochets beautiful, intricate patterns from memory. She knows many complicated origami patterns and draws anything in detail. After barely weeks, she already could play songs on the flute, and I recognized the tunes. And perhaps more importantly, Sivy was eager to learn and sensitive of others.

One evening, at 8:45 P.M., after three hours of doing homework together, Sivy asked, "Are you OK, Mommy?" She was concerned that I was too tired, though she was ready to continue studying.

I was reading the sixth-grade novel *Roll of Thunder, Hear My Cry* aloud to her and explaining it as we read. And every day, I saw less and less frustration and more understanding in her face. She did not need help with math, and she was doing well.

My prayer was that Sivy would know God's unconditional love. I wanted her to know that she was my little girl because of what Christ did; the miracle of her coming to Thailand was a gift from him.

She tried so hard to do everything perfectly, and sometimes I wondered if she feared being sent back if she made a mistake. I didn't know for sure, because Sivy rarely shared her thoughts and feelings during this time. My heart broke when she cried, but she offered no explanation for her deep pain. At those times, I simply held her and loved her unconditionally, even though I didn't know what her tears were about.

I wanted her to read something she would understand and enjoy, so I introduced her to the American Girl books that went with her doll Molly. After a short history lesson about World War II, she enjoyed the stories and took the books to bed with her that night.

Another night, after about three months of living with us, Sivy asked to pray before dinner. "Thank you, Lord, for a good Mommy and a good Daddy, and please help all the orphans in the world. I praise you for helping me to understand English better every day. Amen."

I was blessed beyond measure by this child and wept happy tears.

One Sunday, when we got into the car to go to church, the car wouldn't start. We had a dead battery. Though we were all disappointed, we went into the house to have "home church."

The girls were excited when we said we'd watch the Jesus film. Then shortly after we put in the video, Ed and Ginny, our Thai Buddhist friends, called and asked us to go out to lunch. When they arrived, the

Jesus film still was playing, so we invited them to watch it with us, and Ginny did. Then we went out for a nice lunch at a local Thai restaurant.

When we returned, I shared more about the Lord. Ginny listened politely and acknowledged that Jesus was good for me and that he was a good role model. But she believed she was in control of her destiny and would be fine after death, because she lived well now. During this discussion, Sopheak listened to everything we said.

When our guests had left, Sopheak and Paul went to swim at the nearby pool while Sivy and I read together.

At dinner, the conversation turned back to Jesus. I asked Sivy to tell me about when she first believed in Jesus.

Her dark eyes sparkled as she started her story:

> A woman who worked in the orphanage told me about Jesus first, but I did not believe it. The woman was not nice. Then she left the orphanage and went to work with a church. Later, she came back with people from her church, and they brought help to the orphanage. They taught stories and songs about Jesus.
>
> At first, I did not want to study about Jesus. But as time passed, I began to enjoy the stories and songs. When they got to the story where Jesus told the people to be baptized, I was baptized, and the water was very dirty!
>
> Then Mommy and Daddy came to the orphanage. The director told all the children that two of us would be chosen to go to Thailand to study and live with the teachers. When they were deciding who would go to Thailand, my name was mentioned, and I wanted to go.
>
> I heard Daddy say, "How old is she?" Then I heard him say, "No." At that moment, I went to pray. My heart was so broken. I prayed to Jesus and believed right then.

She wept as she told us this part of the story. I wrapped my arms around her and reassured her that God heard every prayer, and she was chosen by him to come to us.

I was reminded that God also wants us to come to him like children. I was learning so much from these little girls. I still wonder why God allowed me to be part of this miraculous story. And like any mother, I love my girls more than I ever could explain.

Chapter 10

Unconditional Love

SOPHEAK CONTINUED TO be my little Cambodian princess. She was affectionate and craved attention. And since she was a beautiful child, it was easy to love her. When we agreed to take her back to our home in Thailand, I naively thought that all an orphan needed was love, good food, a nice room with a few toys, and clean clothes—but I was wrong. She also needed time to heal, someone to attach to, and a safe place to express her pain.

And as our relationship grew, I became the recipient of Sopheak's affection and also of her frustration. Often, she could not verbalize her frustration or pain, so it was expressed by crying and throwing a fit. She often threw her stuffed toys and tried to push me away during these fits, but I never left her. I held her gently, even when she fought me. And I repeatedly told her I loved her and would never leave. She slowly began to trust; and eventually, I became her safe place.

The small bedroom was feeling crowded for two girls, so we bought bunk beds. Sopheak was thrilled. She chose the bottom bunk and arranged her stuffed animals and dolls across the end of the bed. Her Chinese dragon puppet hung from the bed slats above her. When everything was settled, she propped herself up on the pillows and sat like a princess.

But after about twenty minutes of sheer delight, her expression changed. Her face turned extremely sad, revealing the deep pain. Then she started to cry. I held her, and she hugged me tightly.

I could only imagine what memories flooded her mind. I cried easily with her and told her I wished I could buy every little girl in the world a bed, but I couldn't. God only told me to buy one for her. We wept in each other's arms for a long time.

Several days later, she said, "It is OK. Sometimes Sopheak cry; sometimes Mommy cry."

A week later, she went to bed upset because she did not get to watch a video. It was late, and the day had been too full. She cried hard, but this time she didn't throw her stuffed toys.

When I went upstairs to check on her later, I found her lying in the middle of the bed, without a toy or a pillow. I asked if I could hold her, and she melted in my arms. I wept again and asked God to let me carry some of her pain.

She cried, too, and then said, "Thank you. You are good. I love you because you are good."

Through my tears, I answered, "I love you—all the time."

Unconditional love is a huge lesson for a little orphan girl to learn. I thought, *Lord, give me what it takes to teach such an important lesson. It's a good lesson for mothers, too.*

Several weeks later, the Lord answered my prayer. After church, Paul and I said "no" to an ice cream cone and "no" to candy at the grocery store checkout counter. Then her pout began. While we were in a familiar restaurant, the pout escalated into a fit. Sopheak screamed and wailed and did not want me near her. The closer I came, the louder she cried; we left before we our food was eaten.

When we got home, Paul carried Sopheak into her room. Again, I held her and continually reassured her that we were not going to leave. I prayed, and we both cried. She told Sivy—in their Khmer language—that she didn't want to be held, but when she finally relaxed, she willingly melted in my arms. Paul and I both stayed with her until she was ready to get up, wash her face, and come downstairs to eat.

Later, she hugged me tightly. "Mommy, I love you so much. Thank you, Mommy. I am sorry."

Her apology was from the heart, and she acknowledged that I was hurt when she fought against me. I told her she was forgiven and explained that I loved her when she cried and when she was happy—and so did Jesus.

We had made another connection on an intimate emotional level. We were both growing in ways that we'd never imagined, and it was good. She also had a big hug for Daddy. She ate a good lunch and spent the afternoon with Daddy, working in the wood shop at school.

The next Sunday morning, Sopheak came downstairs dressed in her jeans.

"Jeans are OK, and you can wear them most of the time. But I like something pretty for church," I said. Then I brushed the hair from her face and explained, "I'm old-fashioned."

"What does old-fashioned mean, Mommy?"

I laughed and hugged her. "Old-fashioned means that jeans are OK for church, but I'd rather see you in something pretty."

She ran to her room and came back wearing her butterfly pants and shirt.

By March, we were making great progress toward building our family unit, but it still was not easy. I devoted most of my time to the girls. We spent hours on English lessons and homework. Their smiles and hugs were rewarding, but I often was exhausted.

Sivy tried so hard to do everything perfectly, and she often corrected Sopheak. In the Khmer culture, there is a special word that means to give honor to an older sister. But Sopheak was dropping that title as she learned more English of her own.

In the orphanage, older children always helped discipline the little ones, but we had to teach Sivy that in our home, all the discipline would come from us as parents. We were all stretched in many ways.

Sopheak continued to throw occasional fits, and I never knew what triggered her emotions. But I also continued to sit and hold her as she thrashed around, until she relaxed and wept. Her fits always ended in a tight embrace, a good cry, and a prayer together.

One night when we were in a restaurant, Sopheak cried hard and began the same pattern. When we got her home, she cried for a good hour, which was unusual. In the end, when she finally settled down, she had a headache. She called Sivy and asked her for lotion and a coin. I was shocked as I watched Sivy rub lotion into Sopheak's back and then scrape it with the coin until it left a large, red streak.

Then I had Sivy do it to me, so I'd understand. It didn't hurt, but the marks were horrible.

Sivy continued to "coin" Sopheak's back and chest until the headache subsided. It was hard for me to let her do it, but she assured me that it would help Sopheak feel better.

So we learned another cultural surprise. After that night, the girls discontinued "coining" each other. They learned to ask for Tylenol to relieve a headache, instead.

Chapter 11

They Are Here Now

MONTH BY MONTH we became a family. Through good times and trials, we learned to love and trust each other. Little by little and day by day, the girls became our daughters and sisters to each other. It was not an easy or simple adjustment since they both remembered biological sisters, who were still in Cambodia.

But as we all grew closer, Paul and I knew our next step needed to be officially adopting the girls. It was a big step for all of us, and the girls knew that they would lose some of their Khmer culture over time.

We always encouraged them to speak Khmer to each other. Sivy still read her Khmer Bible. And since Asian food was something we could keep in our Thailand home easily, we did our best to let the girls eat traditional foods, often beginning the day with fish and rice for breakfast.

So I started looking on the Internet for information on foreign adoption. And I contacted Martin in Cambodia and asked for any help he could give. However, every place I looked, the answer was "no." Adoption agencies all said the same thing: "No children are available from Cambodia."

All adoptions between America and Cambodia had been stopped in December of 2002, because of child-trafficking. Martin sent us a copy of Cambodian laws, which stated children could not be adopted in Cambodia after their eighth birthday. Plus, adoptive parents had to be younger than fifty-four years old. And since both girls were older than eight and Paul and I were both older than fifty-four, adoption looked absolutely impossible. Period.

So instead, we decided to apply for the girls to each get a tourist visa to the USA. At the time, our oldest son, Christopher, and his wife, Diana, were in Thailand for a visit, and she used her legal expertise as a lawyer to help us prepare all the documents.

A few days later, we waited our turn outside the US consulate for four hours. Tired yet hopeful, we finally went in to present our paperwork. To prove that we would travel temporarily as tourists and would return to Thailand, we had purchased return-trip tickets for all four of us. We also included our teaching contracts for the upcoming school year.

However, the visas were quickly denied! Not only that, but also we were told that because the girls were Cambodian orphans, they *never* could enter the United States. The laws also stated we *never* could adopt them. And to qualify for a tourist visa, a person had to prove he or she would return to his or her passport country.

We had proven that the girls would return to Thailand, but their passport country was Cambodia. They had no parents, no job, and no money in a bank to ensure a return to Cambodia. The immigration counselor said he was sorry. He believed we were good people, but he had to enforce the US laws, as written.

Now the questions I had tucked in the back of my mind three months ago, when we began this journey, resurfaced with extremely disappointing answers: No, we could not adopt the girls. No, they could not travel to the States.

But some of my fervent prayers were being answered positively: Yes, we were bonding as a family. Yes, the girls were accepting our love. Yes, God was building my faith to be strong enough to accept possible negative answers from the government.

When we left the US consulate that day, I was numb. Our dreams were shattered. They said we never could travel "home" to the States as a family. My own mother never would meet my girls. Paul and I would have to travel separately to visit grandchildren, attend funerals, and celebrate births.

But we knew God had given us these children, and we believed by faith that no government was going to break our family apart. So we cried; we prayed; we praised the Lord. Then we moved ahead with life. We simply planned to remain in Thailand until the girls were raised or until our prayer for a miracle adoption was answered.

Chapter 12

The Gift of Language

SPRING BREAK WAS almost over. We had accomplished loads of English practice, and the girls added words to their vocabularies every day.

We watched the *Anne of Green Gables* videos, which the girls liked. But when Gilbert broke his engagement with the girl he met in college and then got sick, Sopheak was upset. She didn't want Anne and Gilbert to get back together, because he had "had" another woman and now he was sick.

Sopheak explained that in Cambodia, when men have more than one woman, they get sick. They get sores, and their faces turn purple. This led to a discussion about the differences between Gilbert's relationships and the men she referred to in Cambodia.

After four months, their English language ability had improved tremendously, and they could express themselves more openly.

Sopheak prayed one night, "Thank you for Mommy and Daddy, who teach me to obey."

Sivy said, "I have a good life, but I don't know the future."

Sivy said, "I am so happy; I am happier than you."

Sopheak asked, "Daddy, which do you love more, me or America?"

Sivy said, "Hug me like the Tsunami is coming, and you are trying to save me."

Sivy prayed, "Dear Jesus, please help Sopheak to obey Mommy, Daddy, God, and me."

During the first week of May, Sivy asked me what Mother's Day was. She had heard someone talk about it at school. I told her it was a holiday in America, a day set aside to honor mothers. She asked me what "honor" meant. I told her it meant to love, obey, and respect someone.

Then—better than a Hallmark card—she looked at me with her beautiful smile and asked, "Why is it only one day?"

On our first Mother's Day together, we had a special dinner at the Sheraton Hotel. Sopheak ate more at the buffet than I did, and she ate a good variety, trying many new things. She especially loved meat and ice cream.

Since Sopheak wore her princess dress, we visited the hotel's ballroom. It was empty, but she entered like royalty, then twirled and danced and twirled again. Then we rode the glass elevator up and down several times before leaving. Much to our enjoyment, her bright imagination brought everything to life.

After four months of English education, Sopheak expressed herself well. One day, I gave a tour of Grace International School to an elderly couple visiting from the States. They arrived about forty minutes late, and the first thing Sopheak said, after a perfect Thai greeting, was, "Why are you so late?"

Then during the tour, to my surprise, Sopheak asked how old they were. They skirted the answer by saying they were older than I, her mother.

With that bit of knowledge, she asked her next question, "If you are older than my mom, how come your hair isn't gray?"

Later that evening, we had a quick lesson on appropriate questions for visiting Americans!

The school year was coming to an end, but Sopheak was just beginning to read. She could write simple sentences and loved to listen to stories. When I gave a lesson on synonyms to my second graders and asked the class for a word that meant the same thing as "sad," Sopheak's hand started waving wildly. I didn't think she possibly could know the answer, but I decided to give her a chance, so I called on her.

"Forlorn," she said.

My mouth dropped. Then I remembered reading her the story *The House That Jack Built* and, "The maiden all forlorn milked the cow with the coupled horn." Sopheak was the only second grader who knew the meaning of the word "forlorn," and she had been in an English-speaking environment for only five months!

During the final week of second grade, Sopheak was invited to a birthday party. It was her first party, and she was excited. She came downstairs wearing her princess dress and twirled around the living room. The sparkle in her eyes could melt any heart.

"I have a pretty dress, and I have a pretty heart. If the dress gets all dirty, I will still have a pretty heart. My pretty heart is forever," she innocently said, with great wisdom.

I cried again, knowing how important it is for little girls to believe their hearts are pretty, and so grateful to God for giving us the responsibility to care for these precious ones. It's true she was needy and required much of my attention most of the time, but I was accepting her as my own. Moments like this made all the hard work fade away into feelings of pure joy.

Chapter 13

Summer Sadness, Summer Gladness

BY THE END of the school year, we realized that our little house was not adequate for our new family. The girls needed more space, and I wanted a kitchen that was big enough to accommodate several people. I found a great house for rent in the same neighborhood, so we moved in the middle of July.

As I unpacked, I was grateful. But as I thought of my role as mother to the girls, the beautiful house didn't begin to compare to the beauty of their lives. The responsibility of raising them to love and serve the Lord seemed huge, and I felt unworthy. Only the Lord could heal their hurts and fill the emptiness in their young hearts, because they had experienced much more pain than little ones should have to.

"Help me, Lord, to model your love," I prayed.

Soon, school was out for the summer! The girls had completed six months of Western education, and the long nights of homework were behind us for the next ten weeks. But English lessons continued, though in a more informal structure. My instruction was now built simply around stories and word games. Everyone was ready for a break.

Sopheak joined the Tigers Little League team—another new experience. We bought new pink gym shoes for the sport. But she decided to wear her sandals, because she didn't want to get the pretty pink gym shoes dirty. Then she tried unsuccessfully to convince me she could run faster in sandals, anyway.

After only one practice session, they had a game. She went up to bat, hit a line drive, and ran directly to "third" base. Everyone was cheering and laughing at the same time. The coach yelled, "It's all right; put her on first. I didn't teach her which way to run yet." She eventually came around and scored.

In July, the girls received a video from a visiting Cambodian missionary, in their Khmer heart language! After the girls watched it, they wanted me to watch it again with them. I did, while they translated.

The video was produced to help children growing up in hard situations in Cambodia. Many mothers and fathers leave their families to seek employment in the cities there. The message of the film was for children to tell someone if they ever were sexually abused.

I was crying before the video was over because I was afraid of what the girls might tell me now. They are my precious daughters, and I did not want to think that anyone had hurt them. The thought of anyone ever abusing a little girl sickened me. I had never had to deal with anything of that nature before, and I was afraid, for myself and them.

Soon after the video was over, I understood why Sopheak had wanted me to watch it. She began in a childlike way to explain that she had been abused. She was so honest. And she apologized, thinking the abuse might have been her fault because she did not scream.

I reassured her that she was not to blame. I held her and gently whispered assurances that she was pure and innocent and that no little girl is ever to blame if she is abused by an adult. We held each other for a long time, and I encouraged her to keep talking and sharing with me. I told her that I loved her very much.

Later, I prayed, "Lord, thank you for opening her little heart and letting me lead her to you for healing. She is so precious and such a little ball of fire. Let me love her as you do, Lord."

Since the visas to the States were denied, we planned a trip to the beach in the south of Thailand instead. We booked two adjoining rooms in a lovely hotel, that had a large pool and a beautiful view of the ocean. The girls each had their own bed. And since we only had showers at home, they saw a bathtub for the first time. They giggled and splashed in their first bath but insisted on wearing their underwear.

I also wanted them to experience snorkeling that week, so we rented a long-tail boat and a local pilot for one day. Then we headed out to the small islands, under clear skies and beautiful weather. Throughout the day, Sopheak was like a fish in the water with her snorkeling gear. And Sivy tried snorkeling and liked it, until she saw a sea slug and thought it was a giant leech.

Later, the winds picked up quickly, and by mid-afternoon, we were caught in a storm. The ride was rough as we headed back to shore. For about forty-five minutes, the small boat tossed and struggled in the waves, which terrified Sivy. She clutched her seat, shivering and praying. But Sopheak smiled and bounced with every swell. She even wanted to stand up and "catch" the ocean spray.

At one of the local shops the next day, Sopheak had her hair braided and beaded for three hundred and fifty baht ($11.00), while Sivy's longer style would have been more than double at eight hundred baht ($24.00). But she analyzed the idea and said, "I am not a princess. My hair is not worth eight hundred baht." So she chose not to get it fixed. But I gave her three hundred baht to spend on something else, anyway.

Sivy liked to walk the beach with me and collect seashells. We walked often that week and had long talks while resting in the sand. She told me that when the Christians first came to her orphanage, she did not want to learn about Jesus. The staff said she should believe in Jesus when the Christians came, but she could "put Him into a box" when they left.

Sivy liked that idea. She wanted to put Jesus into a box, and then she still could go to the temple for Buddhist holidays and join the celebrations. But she could not tell me in English what the celebrations were for. Thankfully, now she understands that Jesus cannot be "put into a box."

She also quietly shared that she never told her birth mother she loved her. I reassured her that I knew she loved me. Then I explained that she was good at expressing love in more ways than in spoken words, so her mother probably knew too. I have prayed often about this and hope the Lord brings it up again between us. I want the right opportunity to talk with her more about love and ways of expressing it.

Sopheak continued to play in the ocean or the pool all day, every day. She loved the waves and buried herself in the sand more than once. Never shy, she made friends with everyone she met. Like a magnet, she attracted people. The family staying next to us was from Denmark and had two girls her age. When Sopheak first realized the parents spoke English, she immediately and innocently asked, "Are you Christians?"

When she walked the beach, she collected seashells and any plastic garbage that might be useful later. Sopheak loves life and plays hard. One evening, we all played the dice game Pig Mania®, and she kept score. When someone reaches one hundred points, they win, and the game is over. But when Sopheak reached one hundred points, she didn't tell anyone, because she wanted the game to continue—and she would have played all night!

After four days at the beach, Sivy was ready to go home. So when we suggested another boat ride, she cried. I rarely saw tears from Sivy, so this impacted me. Sopheak, on the other hand, begged for another boat trip, but she didn't get her way—not this trip.

On the way home, in the Bangkok airport, without our prompting, Sopheak shared her testimony with a group of Christians who were on their way to Vietnam to work in an orphanage. She spoke of her life in the orphanage before she believed in Jesus and how God had used Papa Tom to lead her to a new Mommy and Daddy.

It seems every time she shares her story in a new context, her wounded heart mends a bit more. And though her energy and zest for life often exhaust me, I am so thankful when I watch her life. Her inner joy brings me to tears.

During the summer break, in small ways, I realized the contrast of sharing deep pain and great joy, both at the same time.

We continued our English lessons every day. I gave Sivy simple writing assignments, and we drilled English grammar. One day she sat working quietly at the dining room table for about an hour. So I asked what she was doing.

"I'm writing a letter to my mother."

"Is it for me?"

"No. It is to my mother who died."

I never have read that letter, because Sivy didn't offer it. I sensed she simply wasn't ready to share it. This part of my little girl emerged often in those early months. She held back much of her internal world.

With Sopheak, however, I always knew exactly what she was thinking and feeling, because she externalized her pain, usually by throwing fits and talking loudly. I loved that about her, because I didn't have to wonder how she felt.

But with Sivy, I often found myself wondering. Our relationship was built on silent moments and shared touches, rather than on words. To this day, I don't know what Sivy did with the letter she wrote to her mother, but I often have prayed that God would use it to bring her healing and bring a bond to our new relationship.

Chapter 14

Pet Parade

ONE DAY SOPHEAK decided she wanted a pet, but I did not want any added responsibilities to my day. And since Paul does not particularly like dogs or cats, we said "no" to the pet request. Then one afternoon, while we were putting cabinets in the kitchen of the larger, empty house we soon would move into, Sopheak found a kitten. It was barely alive, and there was no sign of its mother.

Sopheak loved that tiny kitten and begged to take it home. I told her it needed its mother to survive, and so we must search for the mother. But we couldn't find the cat, so we left the kitten where we found it, hoping the mother would return. Of course, Sopheak was not happy about leaving the kitten, but she obeyed without protest.

Later that night, a big storm blew through, and tree branches flew across the yard. Rain poured, and Sopheak cried as hard because she felt the kitten was getting soaked! Reluctantly, Paul got on his motorbike—in the middle of the storm—and searched for the kitten until he found it. The drenched kitten arrived at our home in a cardboard box. Both were soaked through, so Sopheak wrapped the kitten in a towel for the night.

In the morning it was still alive, so I took it to the vet. He estimated the kitten was barely three weeks old. He prescribed an antibiotic and instructed us to feed it every four hours. Sopheak happily named the kitten Lady, and she attended to it with great care. Lady survived, and Sopheak gave of herself as she loved and fed Lady.

Six weeks later, I woke up to the news that Lady had died. Our maid found her in the road. She had been attacked by a dog. Sopheak cried, kicked, and screamed in my arms for about ten minutes. First she blamed Daddy for leaving our metal gate open, even though Lady easily crawled between the bars. Next she blamed me for not letting Lady sleep with her. Finally, she blamed God for making dogs chase cats.

A few minutes later, with a new thought, she reminded me that the puppy in *101 Dalmatians* was really not dead; it just looked dead. So, maybe Lady wasn't really dead. We unwrapped the towel, and Sophie momentarily put her hand next to Lady's tiny nose.

"I'm not good at this, Mom. You do it."

I leaned over Lady and felt no breath. I confirmed that she was dead. Sopheak cried softly, remembering all the good things about her little Lady. Then she and Paul buried the kitten in a shoebox, in the corner of the yard.

Our mourning period was over in about an hour, when Sopheak came to a new conclusion. "Mom, it's time to buy a new pet. I think I want a puppy. They are stronger."

So that afternoon, we bought Bingo, a cute, little, brown dog with curly fur. He looked like a Beanie Baby® toy. Bingo quickly became a part of our family—even Paul liked him!

Sopheak enjoyed placing Bingo in her bike basket when she rode around the neighborhood. She and Paul also took Bingo in the basket on his motorbike.

He was an adorable puppy, and we all played with him. Sopheak did a great job of taking all responsibility for owning a pet. She fed, groomed, and cleaned up after him willingly.

Then tragedy struck. One day Bingo jumped out of the motorbike basket, and Paul accidently drove over him with both wheels. And unfortunately, Sopheak was on the back of the motorbike that day and witnessed the whole event.

Paul gently picked Bingo up and got them all home as quickly as he could, but Bingo died in his arms. We all cried hard as we prepared a shoebox for his burial. But this time, Sopheak did not blame anyone.

Three days later, we began again with another dog, and Sopheak named her Pollyanna. I enjoy how she retells the story of Bingo's burial: "Mommy cried the hardest, because she loved him the most. Why do puppies have to die?"

But Sivy voiced a strong objection: "This family should not have pets. It is not fair to the animals."

Chapter 15

Provision and Protection

AS SIVY STARTED seventh grade, we still worked through most of her homework together. And though her reading was improving tremendously, I needed to fill in much background knowledge. We talked for hours, and our conversations often shifted from homework to memories.

Sivy shared that she was taken to a "witch doctor" in the village when her knee had its disease. Although she didn't have the words to explain the name of the skin disease, from what I understood, it seemed as if a severe fungus had grown over the skin.

"This looked like cauliflower," Sivy said, rubbing her large scar. "But the witch doctor's plants didn't work, so the woman placed hot, burning wads of cotton on it. They didn't know they were doing harm. They thought they were helping me through the witch doctor. But it was God who moved me to the orphanage and healed my disease. It's OK that I have a scar, because it reminds me of all I learned through it."

I touched her knee gently, as my eyes filled with tears. Then I held her in my arms as she continued.

"The scar is part of me, and it tells a story. It's one of the reasons why I'm here with you. It's my treasure, and it's my testimony. God put it there for a reason, and now I know why."

Sivy also shared that she had lived with a married cousin and his wife while she got medical treatment for her knee in Phnom Penh, after her parents died. While she was there, it was her cousin who decided she should go to the orphanage. He told Sivy she would get medical treatment for her knee, have pretty clothes, and go to a good school.

So she eagerly left for the orphanage, without going back to the village to see her grandmother. But the reality of life at the orphanage was a great disappointment. Sivy confessed to throwing one big fit and crying hard after she arrived. Later, one of her sisters did take her back to visit her grandmother.

Sivy grew spiritually every day. She kept a Bible journal as part of her schoolwork. And as the length of the assigned Bible readings grew, her teacher said I could choose the verses, to make sure she read. But Sivy didn't need that.

"Mom, I always have time to read my Bible."

Her journal was priceless, and she shared it with me. God used her greatly to stretch my own faith. She wrote that she was a descendant of Shem, from the story of Noah, because of her salvation through Christ.

One day Sivy and I were folding clothes and putting them away in her dresser, and she pulled out a small, cloth coin purse with a zipper. She turned to me with a haunted look and then opened it. It contained one hundred US dollars in small denominations. The bills were dirty and folded tightly, to fit in the tiny coin purse. As she laid them in my hand, I asked her where she got the money.

"When my relatives in the village heard I was moving to Thailand, they collected it for me. I was told to use it if I was ever hungry or needed to get back to Cambodia."

I sat silently as I held the money. Then I remembered her telling me previously that her sister warned her to be careful here. She had heard that Cambodian girls often were taken to Thailand and sold.

"But I will not need it. I will give it back someday; it is not my money."

I was beginning to see how naive I was. When Martin first brought the girls to live with us, he had crossed the Cambodian-Thai border with our two young Cambodian girls without question. He obviously had a round-trip ticket, but theirs were both one way here. It's true that all the paperwork was in order for their student visas, but no one at the border even bothered to check. There was no concern for the girls' safety. This proved there was a hole in the security.

Why was a single, white male ever allowed to accompany two young Cambodian girls across the Thai border without even a question? I did not want to comprehend that young girls were sold as slaves. I had nowhere to put that kind of information in the framework of my life experiences.

Since that time, I have learned about the horror of human-trafficking in Southeast Asia. Much of the economic and political stability of this region rests on the shoulders of this crime. I never had thought about these issues, but now they were brought to the forefront of my mind. And I realized how vulnerable my girls had been.

I saw God revealing his plan to me, a little piece at a time. When he asked us to love and educate an orphan, we'd said, "Yes." But we never knew that we'd grow to comprehend an enormous ministry that also needed attention and prayer.

Life in Cambodia

Forty-two orphans call this home.

Children range in age from four to sixteen years.

We meet the girls!

Sopheak and I meet for the first time.

Sopheak passes all informal assessments.

Sivy and I worship together for the first time at the orphanage.

Together we look at the Grace International School yearbook.

Sivy and I met in this kitchen.

Life in the orphanage

Worship time! Only two will leave. The rest will stay behind.

NEW LIFE IN THAILAND

English lessons started immediately with picture books—another new experience!

Sidewalk chalk is a new experience.

The girls get their first bikes!

First days of school

Dressed for the first day of school

Sixth grade includes music lessons for Sivy on the flute.

Second grade includes lessons in English and math for Sopheak.

BEAUTY FROM THE INSIDE OUT!

One year later, the girls are adjusting well!

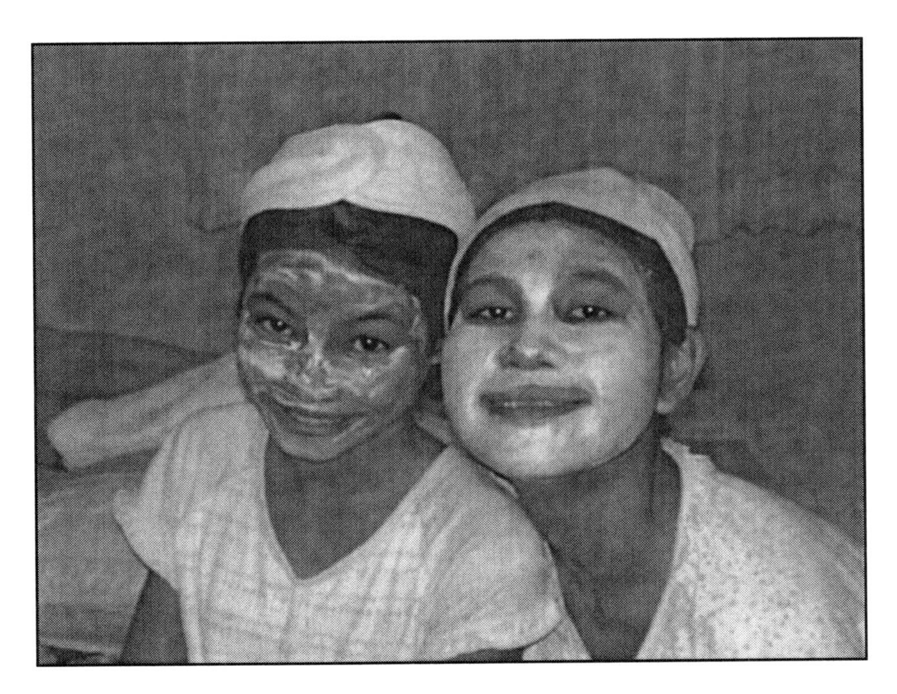

The masks are gone! The smiles are contagious!

Family vacations

The beach in Thailand is always a favorite vacation spot!

Another first experience-when we visit America.

Cambodian adoption

Miracles do happen! The Cambodian adoption is complete on March 2, 2007.

The blue fingers lighten the mood of a stressful adoption!

"This is my Cambodia!"

Sivy and I walk the fields of her childhood.

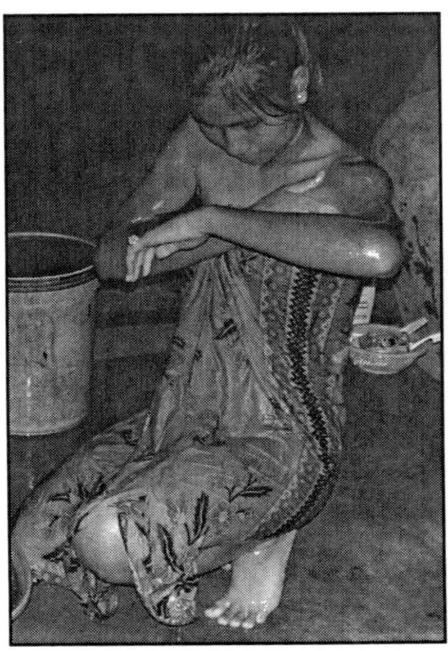

Sivy gracefully demonstrates how to bathe at the pump!

Sisters put on a style show with traditional Khmer clothes.

Sopheak learns to swim

AND DEVELOPS INTO A CHAMPION!

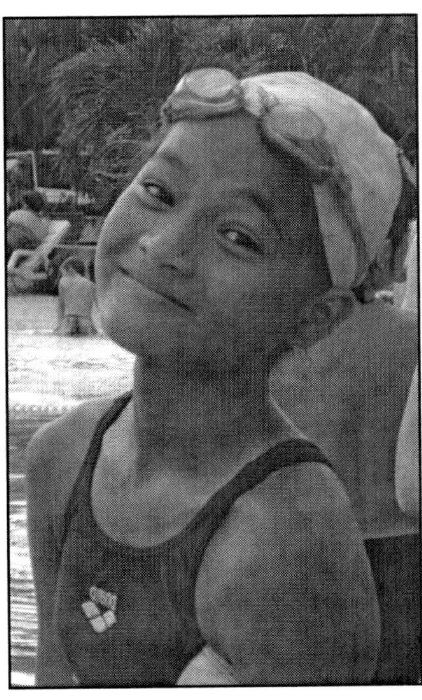

Life in Thailand…

Always includes a trip to the Elephant Camp.

Learning how to cook Thai style

Our wait in Hawaii

US history lessons start at Pearl Harbor.

April 1, 2009—Sivy and Sopheak Jarot are US citizens.

Chapter 16

A Daughter's Forgiveness

ONE DAY WHEN Sivy didn't have much homework, she was excited to get out her crocheting. As she stitched, she casually talked about her past. She remembered her father teaching her to use a spoon. Her mother taught her how to crochet when she was little and even whittled her first crochet hook out of a piece of wood. Then when Sivy got to the orphanage, she learned more fancy stitches.

She talked about working alongside adults in the rice paddies during the three stages of planting and the backbreaking task of harvesting. Her many memories included her older sisters and brother teasing her because she was afraid of leeches that clung to her ankles as she walked through the water-filled rice fields.

Sivy remembered a Cambodian missionary who had talked with her about being a Christian. One family in her village had claimed to be Christian. Her understanding of Christianity at that time was how believers celebrated when someone died, and how they buried their dead instead of cremation. Then, as she talked and crocheted a while, she eventually shared that her mother once heard about Jesus but said the stories were not true.

One day, Sivy's teacher gave her the assignment of writing fifteen major events from her family history, starting with her grandparents. From this information, she had to create a timeline. Then, finally, she was to give an oral report on one event that had shaped her family's life the most.

When Sivy read over this assignment, she started to cry. I asked her why. Was she crying because the assignment was hard? Or was it because the things she would have to write were painful? She said it was both.

I held her as she wept gently and reassured her that it was OK to cry. The pain she felt was very real.

After a good hug, she wiped her eyes. "I can do it, Mom."

A half hour later, she came down stairs with the report written. And over the next week, Sivy practiced her oral report. She shared that her father once made a big mistake. When he went to war, he was with another woman. When he came back to the family, he had HIV, but he did not know it. He soon became very sick and passed the disease on to her mother.

When her father died, Sivy shaved her own head, as a sign of respect. She watched his body burn in their yard, as he was cremated, and she solemnly spoke of forgiveness for her father. Then she talked about how she cared for her mother until she, too, died of AIDS.

These are examples, to me, of a level of forgiveness that I have not known.

"Lord, thanks for my little daughter's example and for healing her sweet heart."

Chapter 17

A Thankful Heart

SOPHEAK STARTED THIRD grade and chattered all the time. Her grammar improved and so did her vocabulary. One weekend, we made doll clothes, and I introduced the word "gather" as I put the puffed sleeves on a dress. I explained that it meant to come together.

"I know," Sopheak said. "Penguins gather together on the ice to keep warm."

Later that night, she explained to Sivy what a fawn was and described a deer. And as she talked, she shared more of her past—mostly good memories.

> I was about four years old when my mom took me to the dump for the first time. The dump was full of junk; it was smelly and dirty. I was going there because my family needed food. When we got there, it started to drizzle. So my mom found an old couch and a tarp. She covered me with the tarp as I sat on the couch. She cared for me and did not want me to get wet. Then she told me to stay right there. I was not to go anywhere. She left to find food and anything else that we might need.
>
> The dump was near a forest, and that was the way she headed. I did not know what was in the forest or what could happen to her.

> I waited and waited and waited for so long. It seemed like forever. Then suddenly the rain stopped, and she came out of the forest. I felt relieved and comforted to see her again. She had food and some other things we might need later.

The idea of self-sacrifice as a form of love came up often. One time, she noticed that the little girl who lived in a shack down the street had better clothes than her parents. Sopheak told me how good that was.

"Her parents must love her."

Sopheak remembers she had three mommies and two daddies, but she's not positive.

"One mommy did not want me. She put me in the garbage. I don't remember, but my sister told me."

"If that is true, it's a sad thing," I assured her. "Mommies are not supposed to do that. And I would never do that to you. And you must always remember, God will never do that to you."

The longer the girls were with us, the more we talked about adoption and visas and permanent legal guardianship. Sopheak referred to all this paperwork as "special papers." I never knew how much she understood at ten years old, but she always listened and silently processed the information.

One time she crawled into my lap, as she often does. "Mommy, I am thankful that America won't give special papers to Cambodian children."

"Why are you thankful for that?"

"Because if there were special papers, Papa Tom might be my daddy, and I wouldn't be here with you and Daddy. I want you and Daddy."

As I cried, I realized how amazed I am at the depth of this little girl's insights.

Sopheak chose to stay home with Daddy one evening and watch a video while I went shopping at the Night Bazaar. When I came home, she and Paul were still snuggled on the sofa. *The Little Princess* was coming to the end, where Sarah had found her father.

Then Sopheak began to cry and crawled onto Paul's lap. "You two are very good. I love you because you are nice, you are kind, you don't fight each other, and you won't take me back to the orphanage."

We saw our little princess healing from the inside out, expressed by her gratitude and trust. And we vowed that she was absolutely correct; we never would take her back to the orphanage! Thank you, Lord.

Chapter 18

A Tiny Step Forward

THE FOLLOWING SCHOOL year, even though the girls were well into third and seventh grade, I still read almost everything aloud to them, and they comprehended more and more. They enjoyed school and never complained about the hours of homework. But their learning to read and write English was more than a full-time job for all of us.

We kept in contact with Martin in Cambodia and sent letters and report cards to the director of the orphanage. The girls had been with us now for eight months. And we realized more than ever, we wanted to pursue their legal adoption.

But as we read and reread the copy of the adoption laws from Cambodia, they made no sense! These girls needed a home, and we were willing to provide one. But the law stated that no children over the age of eight could be adopted and that no adult over fifty-four could adopt them. We definitely failed in both requirements!

A small bit of encouragement came from Martin, when he explained that we could file a petition through the Cambodian government. We could first become the girls' legal guardians. The orphanage director was the legal guardian then, and he agreed to let us apply and change the guardianship from his name to ours. The papers that we had prepared and signed at the orphanage when we first agreed to take the girls had granted us only temporary guardianship. They allowed the girls to attend school. So we agreed Martin should file the new paperwork, and we prayed.

One day after church, several months later, we made a call to the orphanage in Cambodia for Sivy. She and Sopheak talked to people for about fifteen minutes. Then they came running out to the porch.

"We got the special papers!" Sopheak shouted. She understood that we received "special papers," though she didn't comprehend what that meant.

I quickly got in touch with Martin, who slowly explained that the Cambodian government only gave legal permission for the girls to live and study in Thailand. They refused to name us their permanent guardians. And since applying for legal custody is the first step for the adoption process in Cambodia, this rejection confirmed the fact that they would not allow us to adopt the girls.

But Sopheak insisted that we celebrate the "special papers," and I agreed. My mind raced ahead, thinking of what we could do to celebrate this moment in their lives. It hadn't gone exactly as we'd hoped. Then the Lord prompted me to ask, "What would you girls like to do to celebrate?"

"We should take a walk as a family with our puppy. And then maybe we could play a game!" Sopheak said enthusiastically.

I learned another lesson. Sopheak celebrated the "best" of the moment, finding pleasure and contentment in our present situation.

And though we obviously were disappointed about not to be given legal guardianship, we still rejoiced in our blessing: the girls legally lived with us. And we could travel between Thailand and Cambodia with them any time.

"They are here for now!" Paul added as encouragement.

Chapter 19

Call Me Sophie

OUR FIRST GRANDDAUGHTER, Lucille Scout Jarot, was born on September 19, 2005. I had to decide whether to stay with our girls in Thailand and not see Lucy or leave them for the first time and travel to America. But since I was eager to be "Grandma" for a few weeks, I prayed and asked for direction. I knew that my son and daughter-in-law were capable of caring for their new baby without me, but I wanted to see my first granddaughter!

It was a big step for me to leave the girls, but the Lord impressed on my heart that they were ready to spend time with their dad. So I made plans and bought tickets to Chicago.

We had pizza together at the airport before I left for my week-long trip. Then we stood in a huddle and prayed. Then I left my girls for the first time. We all would miss each other. But as they turned and walked away, holding Paul's hands, I knew they were ready.

I enjoyed every minute of being Grandma, but I also was eager to go home to be Mom again. I'd never realized how much I would miss my girls.

When I arrived back at the Chiang Mai airport, Sopheak jumped into my arms. Sivy waited her turn, then hugged me long and hard—as if she never would let go.

How I had missed them! But Paul assured me that they did fine, and the time he'd spent alone with them had been great. Then I asked Sopheak if Daddy had taken good care of her.

"Yes. And he is getting better at it every day," she said.

On October 31, 2005, we decided to celebrate. Only one year prior, Paul and I had reunited with Tom Patrick at the Sizzler® restaurant. So we took the girls out to lunch after church. And we were able to sit at the exact same table where we had met Tom the year before. Wow! God had done wonders in all of our lives during the past year. He had created a family, healed wounded hearts, and filled our deepest desires with himself.

One day not long after, when Paul, Sopheak, and I were driving to Sivy's soccer game, Sopheak asked what book I was reading.

"This book is helping me to be a better mom to my adopted girls."

"That's not a good thing to do," she said and frowned.

"Why?"

"It won't work. Books aren't magic."

"What should I do to make sure I am being the best mom I can be?"

"You should pray. And if you want to read a book, you'd better start with the Bible."

Paul almost drove off the road!

Sopheak continued to progress in third grade. Her spoken English was good, but she was still in beginning readers. So during the day, she worked with a modified third-grade curriculum. At night and on weekends, I taught her a combined first-and second-grade course. She remained eager to learn and remembered everything.

But frustration hit when her classmates, teachers, and even sometimes her mom could not pronounce her Khmer name "correctly." So after she had been with us for about a year, she said she wanted to permanently use a nickname that everyone could pronounce: Sophie—a perfect fit!

One day her third-grade teacher gave her a fact sheet to complete for her autobiography. But it brought her to tears. She said, "Nobody knows about my birth."

She did not know her birth mother's name. And she once said her father was basically called "Pig." I told her not to worry about the spaces she couldn't fill in. But she insisted on doing as much as she could. Then, she decided to begin writing her autobiography at the time of her new life with us.

It still upset her not knowing what year she was born. And she thought no one really knew. So we decided she should count backwards, ten years from 2005, and that would be her birthday year.

"That is why I need you in third grade!" she exclaimed, as her pretty eyes lit-up with excitement.

Later, her completed report earned an "A." It had been a painful process, but the Lord used it to help heal her more.

Chapter 20

First Trip Back

BARELY AROUND THE corner was Christmas, and this year, I wanted to start some traditions for our new family. I shared the legend of the Christmas stockings with the girls and then sewed them each a special one. Sophie was so enthralled with the idea that she made another stocking out of paper and yarn. She hung it over her bed with a sign that read, "Please put something in here." Her daddy filled it.

Christmas marked the anniversary of the girls' arrival in Thailand. So once again, my son Nathan and his wife, Lisa, came from the States and joined us for a special celebration. We all planned to travel into Cambodia, where we'd visit the girls' orphanage and Sivy's family in their village.

The girls didn't know that Nathan and Lisa were coming, nor did they know about the trip to Cambodia. We planned to put the plane tickets in their Christmas stockings—an early Christmas surprise.

Nate and Lisa arrived at the airport, and then we took them directly to the school's playground, to meet Sophie at recess. When she saw them, she ran and jumped into Nathan's arms. What an expression of joy! She hugged Lisa and introduced all her third-grade friends. The rest of the children gathered around to see what all the excitement was about.

Sophie stood tall and confident and talked a mile a minute, explaining her third-grade world to Nate and Lisa. When it was time to go back to class, she skipped happily away.

Sivy was in the cafeteria at this time, so I found her and said I had a surprise. When Nathan and Lisa walked up behind me, Sivy got tears in her eyes. Then she gave them a big hug and shyly said, "I don't like surprises."

Her eyes sparkled as she began to understand that Nate and Lisa were there to visit a while, and they let it slip that we were all going to Cambodia together. Sivy peppered me with questions, until I told her the whole plan. Then she finished her school day on an emotional high, earning a perfect score on a math test.

Before leaving for Cambodia, we bought gifts for the orphans. My son Christopher, his wife, Diana, and her family also helped. They decided not to buy gifts for each other that year. Instead, they sent the money with Nate so we could use it for the orphanage.

But we had a bit of a challenge keeping ten-year-old Sophie focused on taking practical gifts. Instead, she chose sparkly hair clips and party dresses as gifts for her Cambodian friends. And she insisted that everything be beautifully wrapped. She wanted to share nice things from her new world with her little orphan friends. I prayed constantly that she was ready for this trip.

Sivy and Sophie were both so excited. The night before we flew, Sophie rolled her hair in curlers, so she would look extra pretty on her big day.

Soon we were packed and off to the airport. We were all given special stickers to wear, indicating that we would change terminals from domestic to international.

Everything was fine—until we got to Bangkok. Sophie's sticker was coming off her clothes, and I tried to help keep it on. But by that point, she was on emotional overload and started to have a fit.

My mind filled with many doubts. Had I made a mistake? Was she not ready for this trip? Was she afraid we would leave her at the orphanage? She did not cry out loud, and she was extremely observant of her surroundings.

We went to Burger King in the airport, where I sat close to her, confining her movements to a corner seat in a booth. She cried quietly and gave me unpleasant looks. But she did not scream. The others in our group left us alone to work it out—and we all prayed fervently. At that point, I really did not think we would make it to Cambodia.

Then Sophie unexpectedly settled down, gained her control, and simply continued to weep quietly. Barely minutes before our boarding time, she melted in my arms and apologized to everyone. Within minutes, we were all seated on the plane. More answered prayers.

In Cambodia, Martin met us at the airport, with a van full of squirming children from the orphanage. They were so excited to see Sivy and Sophie. Immediately, Sivy engaged them in conversation. But Sophie stood close to me and looked for reassurance before she greeted her friends. After about ten minutes, our families left the children and checked in to a small hotel. We were ready for a quiet meal together and a good night's rest.

The next morning, we walked a few blocks, searching for a tuk-tuk to hire for the day. Sophie was bothered each time she saw small children without a mother. She wanted everyone cared for, and she insisting we give generously to beggars.

"Where is that little girl's mommy?"

"They are hungry, Mom."

We rode through the normal, crowded, dirty streets to visit the girls' previous orphanage home, and Sophie saw the city with new eyes.

"Why doesn't somebody clean this place up? If I was the prime minister, I would make it against the law to throw garbage on the street!"

I told her to save that thought. Maybe someday she *would* be the Prime Minister of Cambodia.

When Sophie walked into the orphanage, she continued to stand very close to me, while the children waited silently at a distance. Then she looked up at me and asked, "What do I do now?"

"Go and play!"

She looked at me again for a bit of reassurance, then stepped forward and played with several of her old friends. We visited the orphanage three times that trip, and each time she asked if she could spend the night with them. Each time, I said, "No." When she asked why, I explained that we were a family now, and families stay together. She never questioned my answer, but it was interesting that she still asked to stay every time we visited.

While we were there, we were introduced to Sophie's aunt, uncle, and two young cousins. One little cousin now lived in the orphanage because her mother could not provide for her. I learned that the family lived near the dump and collected garbage for a living. I assumed this was one of the aunts Sophie had lived with. And because I was not sure of how strong the relationships might still be, I never let Sophie out of my sight. She did not seem excited to see this aunt, but she did enjoy playing with her cousin.

It is customary for extended families in Cambodia to assist each other financially, so the aunt asked Sophie for money. I also noticed she was pregnant, and we willingly helped her.

One day, we took the entire group of orphans to the riverfront to tour the king's palace and take a boat ride on the Mekong River. Everyone was excited, and we invited Sophie's aunt and uncle to come also. Sophie did not pay much attention to her aunt but spent most of her time with her old friends from the orphanage. She also found communicating a bit frustrating, because she had lost some of her Khmer language.

Sivy's sister Rachany hurried to the orphanage to visit, after work at a nearby garment factory. The reunion brought tears to us all, which quickly changed to shouts of joy from the girls. Sivy and Rachany share the same radiant smile. They giggled and hugged as they talked. And

Sivy was quick to share her love for Jesus and expound on her new life in Christ.

The next day, we left early in the morning for Sivy's village. We traveled three hours in a rented van. And the bumpy, winding roads, combined with unique smells and the unfamiliar breakfast, all made me carsick. Though I wanted to savor every moment of Sivy's reunion with her family, I spent most of the day flat on my back, on the floor in her grandmother's small, wooden house.

Numerous aunts and uncles greeted our van as we pulled into the dirt yard. Everyone hugged Sivy immediately. Paul and I received respectful Khmer greetings. Many aunts and uncles prepared food to share with us, but I did not recognize anything except rice. I was still sick from the car ride, so I excused myself as the others sat on the floor of the house and ate family-style.

When I felt a bit stronger, Sivy and I took a walk through the village. It was a wonderful time together. I met Rachana, Sivy's eldest sister, and her husband. Sivy showed me the rice field she used to tend and the road she'd walked to school. She showed me the house where the "Christians" lived and spoke politely to everyone. She loved her country and the open fields spotted with an occasional palm tree. But since my stomach was still quite upset, I visited every outhouse along the way. I remember being in one with a live chicken—and no toilet paper—for quite a while! Sivy held my hand as we walked, and our relationship deepened as she shared her world with me.

We traveled back to Phnom Penh late that night. It had been a full day, but I was thankful to experience a taste of the cultural gap that my girls had to bridge.

On Christmas Eve, we invited Sivy's sister Rachany and a friend to stay overnight in the hotel with us. We rented a room for the three girls to be together and visit more. But when Sivy later asked to sleep in her sister's rented room, we said, "No, you should stay with our family." But her sister was thrilled to enjoy a hotel with a shower, a TV, and bed sheets.

Early on Christmas morning, we attended a large evangelical service in town. The music was lively, and the message included a dramatic presentation of the Christmas story. It was in Khmer and well done; the salvation message was clearly given. Then Rachany walked forward to express her belief in Christ as her Savior, and we all prayed and praised the Lord. We spent the rest of the day, including Christmas dinner, at the orphanage with all the kids. It was refreshing to see the children so thankful for simple gifts and beef stew.

On December 27, 2005, we arrived home in Thailand. Nate and Lisa were already on their flight back to America. The girls had been with us for a full year, and now we'd made a complete circle by visiting Cambodia.

But Sivy soon expressed concern for her sister's new faith. "Can we be sure she is a Christian? How will she learn about Jesus without a Christian teacher? She has to work on Sundays and cannot go to church. Is that OK?"

I assured her that Rachany was a Christian and that God would not leave her. It was our job to pray, and God would provide spiritual food for her. Then Sivy reflected on how the visit had changed her.

> My experience in the orphanage in Cambodia taught me life lessons, and it affects my life today. After living in the orphanage for two and a half years, I realized how I had improved while living in that place. I learned to be humble and accept what the orphanage offered me. I did not know what to expect for my future back then. And I was afraid to expect anything great for myself, because I realized that things don't always turn out to be what I expected.
>
> God eventually gave me a new family. He brought me so far from the orphanage and gave me much more than I expected. Living with my adoptive parents in Thailand and going to a wonderful Christian school is a great privilege and blessing for me. Coming from a place of nothing to a place of everything, I am grateful for all I have.

I am thankful for the unique experience I had in my poor orphanage in Cambodia. It was not the most wonderful experience in my life, but I'm sure glad I had it, because it taught me many life lessons. It humbled me and reminds me to be thankful for what I have today. Like the apostle Paul said, a person really knows how to live when there aren't many things and when there are plenty of things. I know what he meant. I'm the same.

Chapter 21

Miracle

OUR FIRST YEAR together had passed quickly, though we were challenged in many ways. Mixing two cultures was not easy, but we worked to recognize and cling to the best of both. And learning the English language was still hard, as the girls now competed with peers in grades three and seven.

They both strived for excellence, and I read assignments to them every night. I was tired, so very tired, but the girls continued to grow and learn, and their English improved daily.

By the middle of the school year, I was no longer reading Sivy's novels to her, and her math was excellent. She was confident and tried many new activities; she played soccer and basketball for the first time. Music became an important part of her life as she sang and played her flute.

Sophie quickly became a writer, able to express herself through strong verbal skills. She loved her third-grade teacher and always did her best. She was confident and did not realize she was reading below the rest of the class. She made many friends and filled her life with activity.

Paul and I decided that our hearts were totally prepared to stay in Thailand with the girls. Yet we prayed for a miracle that would let us travel to the States with them. But we also were determined that if we had to stay in Thailand until they were grown, we were content to do so.

Chiang Mai is a safe city in which to raise a family, and Grace International School provided much cultural diversity. Sivy and Sophie enjoyed each year's return to visit Cambodia, but they never would return permanently to live the life of their village, the dump, or their orphanage. So we lived daily and waited content to live where God had placed us.

Then a miracle arrived on July 29, 2006, through an email from Martin:

> In Phnom Penh I met for coffee with the director of the orphanage and Mr. Run, an important figure in the Cambodian government, who works closely with Prime Minister Hun Sein. We have prayed for a miracle, and I guess this is one!
>
> We sat down, and Mr. Run said, "I have heard about how you help the children of Cambodia and that you brought two of them to study in Thailand. What can I do to help you?"
>
> I explained the situation and how badly you guys want to adopt the two girls and give them the best opportunity possible to excel and develop to their full potential.
>
> Mr. Run then answered, "Wow! Can you do more of this? Do you know others wanting to do the same?"
>
> He went on to explain, "According to the legal system and the Cambodian adoption laws, this case is not possible, mostly because of the girls' ages. But, I would love to do whatever I can to see this become a reality."
>
> Since it's a special case, you will need to plead to Prime Minister Hun Sein for approval. It could be possible. We do not need to do a case visitation in Thailand, because you already have most of the needed paperwork and proofs. But in addition, you need to provide these things:

1. A letter to Mr. Prime Minister Samdech Hun Sein, Phnom Penh, The Kingdom of Cambodia, from Grace International School,

explaining the case. Also, have them write about the two girls: how long they have studied there, their motivation, attitudes, progression, grades, social adaptation, how tuition fees are paid, and their grades.

2. A short statement from the US Embassy in Bangkok, stating that they would approve visas for the two girls if the Cambodian government approves the adoption.
3. A letter to Mr. Prime Minister Samdech Hun Sein, Phnom Penh, The Kingdom of Cambodia, from the Jarots. Introduce yourselves and explain who you are, educational degrees, occupations, etc.

   Explain your connection to Cambodia and how you met the girls. How did you feel when you met the children? Explain your research on the adoption laws, how you found that the two girls don't fit, and that the second-best thing you could do was to provide a scholarship to study at Grace International School. Make it a personal, heartfelt letter.
4. If possible, send a letter from an American senator to Prime Minister Hun Sein, supporting the case."

We were so excited about this email! God was opening a door, and we were going to step through it joyfully. We felt that we easily could provide everything the Cambodian government wanted, except the letter from our US Embassy, granting visas.

We had been told that the girls never would get visas to American because they were Cambodian orphans and could not prove that they would return to their passport country. But they had no ties to Cambodia, no address, no bank accounts, no jobs. So we continued to pray for another miracle.

Chapter 22

God Opens the Door

THE NEXT DAY, we all got in our car and drove to the American Consulate. Since God had opened this door, we decided to go, tell them our story, and ask for a letter explaining the American laws on adoption and visas.

When we got through security and finally spoke to someone behind a glass window, we simply told our story. This counselor became interested in our dilemma. He checked our file and told us that there was no record of the girls being denied tourist visas.

This was strange to us, because we knew they had been denied. The counselor explained that the application never was officially processed. It still was waiting in the computer. We quickly realized this was to our advantage.

He asked us questions about the length of time we had lived in Chiang Mai and our occupations. He did some research and printed out the laws for immigrant visas. "It doesn't look good," he said sadly. "But it's the man behind the window who makes the final decision on tourist visas."

As we got ready to leave, he shook our hands and said, "Good luck. I told you everything you need to know."

When we left and were outside of the consulate, I said to Paul, "I think he just told us to reapply for tourist visas."

So we headed directly to school and the nearest computer to complete new applications for tourist visas. We paid the fee required and got an interview appointment for August 7, 2006.

Then we returned to the consulate on the designated date. And a few hours later, we exited the building with a "Tourist visa" stamped in each girl's Cambodian passport!

It turns out that the officer who helped us was only on a temporary assignment in Chiang Mai. We truly believe that God put him there especially to help us, because he soon left that position, barely a few days after he issued our visas. He was our angel.

Finally, now we could make photocopies of the visas in the girls' passports and send them with the other documents to the Prime Minister of Cambodia. It was all too good to be true. We had everything we needed to plead for these two Cambodian adoptions. And I was going to travel to America with my girls for the first time!

School was starting in a week, but we would not be there; we were flying to America! I was thrilled to know that my family and friends could finally meet our girls.

Chapter 23

Great Joy, Deep Grief

THE NEXT DAY, my niece Kristin called and told me my sister Claudia was dying. Her cancer had returned and had attacked her spinal column. And I realized how clearly the Lord knew why we needed those visas.

I didn't want Claudia to die without meeting my girls. I prayed for God's perfect timing and was able to leave for America the very next day. Paul and the girls would follow me as soon as he could buy tickets and make arrangements.

I saw Claudia in the hospital, immediately after I landed in the States. She recognized me, but she couldn't talk. She was on a lot of pain medicine, but she knew I was there and opened her eyes to respond. The next few days were hard, as I watched her fade away. But one of my best memories includes reading everything she had underlined in her Bible. Each day, whenever I'd stop reading, my mother, in the chair next to me, asked me to continue, and that was a gift.

Four days later, I met Paul and the girls at the airport. We all drove to Nathan's house to sleep; we all were exhausted.

The next morning, we headed quickly to Claudia and Larry's house, since she had been moved home from the hospital the previous day. She always had wanted to die at home. And though I had so desperately wanted my sister to meet my sweet girls, she died a half hour before they arrived. The girls saw her body as the hospice nurse bathed her, and someone had already called the morgue. This was God's perfect timing, but I was extremely sad.

During the next four weeks, we traveled. First we went to Florida to spend time with my mother. Then we went to North Carolina to visit our son Michael, his wife, Andrea, and their boys. It was a whirlwind of activity and mixed emotions.

By the middle of September, we were back in Thailand, finishing preparations on the paperwork to submit to Cambodia for the official petition for Sophie and Sivy's adoption.

I still was grieving the loss of my sister, but I had to move forward quickly with the petition to the prime minister. I wrote him the following letter:

1 September 2006
Dear Prime Minister Hun Sein,

We, Paul E. and Paula M. Jarot, request permission to adopt Sopheak Chheang and Sivy Meas. Both girls have been living with us in Chiang Mai, Thailand, and attending Grace International School since December, 2004. We believe that God brought these girls to us, and we love them as our own. They are gifted in many ways and have brought great joy to our hearts.

My husband and I are both educators with Master Degrees and have been teaching at Grace International School since 1997. Prior to this, we taught in Papua New Guinea and the USA. Because of our love for children and our years of teaching experience, the girls adjusted quickly to their new home and school. We've taught many lessons around the dinner table, in addition to their formal education in the classroom.

In November of 2004, we met a missionary doctor who had done medical work at the orphanage in Phnom Penh. He told us of a special child whom he believed had great potential. He asked us to pray about bringing her to live with us and attend Grace International School.

On December 5, 2004, we traveled to Phnom Penh to visit the orphanage and meet Sopheak Chheang. When we first met Sopheak, she exhibited a joy for life and an eagerness to learn. We watched her play with her peers and organize games; she laughed and ran and was a healthy child. Her school uniform was clean, and she quickly took responsibility of changing to her play clothes. The orphanage had done a good job of nurturing the children.

While we were making arrangements for Sopheak to come to Thailand to study, we were encouraged to take another child also. This way, the children could keep their Khmer language and be a help to each other. Then we met Sivy. She was one of the older girls and had a small amount of English. We watched her as she served the other children and wore a smile that came from deep inside. Again we saw a gifted child who needed a chance to become all she was meant to be.

We prayed and started the paperwork for passports and visas to Thailand for the girls. Twenty days later, they arrived in Chiang Mai, and our new family started. It has been almost two years since the day they arrived. We can't imagine our lives without them. We love the girls as our own.

We have three married sons, and they and their wives have all met the girls. They have embraced both Sopheak and Sivy as their little sisters. We will raise our daughters as we did our sons and provide good medical care, a loving environment, and a good education. After they graduate from Grace International School, we will provide opportunities for them to continue their education in the area of their choice.

Because of our commitment to teach in Thailand, we will raise the girls in an Asian culture. We want them to continue to understand and appreciate their heritage. They both have many strong Asian characteristics that show in their good work ethics, respect of others, and creative artistic talents. We want to help them develop these gifts.

Thank you very much for taking time to consider our request.

Sincerely,
Paul and Paula Jarot

All the required documents were now ready, and we included two extra letters. Each girl wrote personally to the prime minister and asked for permission to be adopted by the Jarots. Sophie wrote hers in English, and Sivy wrote in beautiful Khmer script.

We checked and rechecked each document; then Paul mailed them. I couldn't help but remember those ominous words we had heard over and over again: "It is simply impossible for Americans to adopt Cambodian children." But I knew that God was driving this process, and He didn't necessarily have to conform to either American or Cambodian laws.

We prayed; we waited. And to our great delight, astonishment, and blessing, the Cambodian prime minister approved both adoptions! We worship the God of miracles! October 26, 2006, was a day to celebrate. The adoptions would not be final until a court date was set in Phnom Penh, when we would all have to be present for the ceremony.

According to the adoption laws in Cambodia, a child cannot be adopted after the age of eight—yet our girls were eleven and fifteen. But because these adoption requests went directly to the prime minister, he was able to approve them personally, which was our huge step forward.

Chapter 24

Back to the Village

AS WE GOT ready to celebrate the second anniversary of the girls' arrival, we planned a quiet Christmas at home. Never did I suspect the adventure that awaited us—barely around the corner.

Sivy's brother called to say that her grandmother was deathly ill, and they wanted Sivy to come back to her village. Paul and I thought it was important that she see her grandmother again, so we immediately purchased tickets for Sivy and me to return alone. Sophie would stay home with Daddy.

Sivy had yearned and prayed for an opportunity to share her faith with her grandmother. So she became eager for this trip. However, the day we were scheduled to depart for Cambodia, we received another phone call. Grandmother had died. Sivy wept in my arms.

We flew out the next day, anyway, and went to her village. I was with Sivy and her siblings when her grandmother's casket was opened for the final viewing. As a sign of respect and mourning, Sivy and her sisters wore black skirts and white blouses, while her brother and uncle dressed in white. Everyone present wore a black patch pinned to their shirts.

When I saw how everyone had dressed, I quickly changed from my jeans to a white T-shirt and black, cropped pants. When I packed, I was thinking "village," not "funeral." But this special occasion required the proper clothes, just as my culture did, and I realized I still had so much to learn about my girls.

Neighborhood men carried the casket from the house and placed it on a cart in the yard, under a white canopy. Sivy, her siblings, and her uncle pulled the cart by a long, thick, white cord.

The girls handed flowers to everyone as an elder from the village lit incense and led the procession. I walked behind the cart with a large group of villagers. And I could see Sivy, far in the front, her head lifted to the sky. My beautiful child stood tall and erect as she walked, and I knew she was praying. She loved her grandmother so much, and yet it was obvious that she loved her Lord even more.

I prayed as we walked about a mile through the rice fields to the temple, where the village elders soon would prepare the casket to be burned, along with the white cord and canopy. After that ceremony was finished, we all went back to the house to eat the special funeral foods; the only thing I recognized was rice. But to be respectful and polite, I took small spoonsful of several dishes, which I thought were vegetables. I quietly avoided the "mystery meats."

Several hours later, the family was called back to the temple. The grandmother's remains lay on a large, metal tray and were carefully pulled away from the crematorium onto the grass. Some of the older men poured water over the ashes, which produced steam on the hot metal. I felt totally out of place as I watched and took pictures. Sivy assured me everything was fine. The entire process seemed so routine to everyone else and yet so strange to me.

A small altar constructed of sticks, leaves, and grass stood about ten feet from the tray that contained the remains of Sivy's grandma's body. One person placed a large banana leaf on top of the remains. Then one-by-one, the elders arranged money in the shape of a person upon the leaf. They said prayers, chanted, and burned incense. Then they dragged the banana leaf off the remains and over to the altar, where a small serving of food and incense burned. As some of the men chanted and waved the burning incense, sparks flew and caught portions of the grass on fire. This changed the mourners' mood, as everyone laughed, jumped around, and stamped out the fires.

But the quick change from the somber ceremony to a comedy scene made me feel uncomfortable. So Sivy explained that they believed Grandma's spirit had to travel from the bones that remained in the ashes to the altar. Once that was done, her children and grandchildren picked the bones and teeth from the ashes. Sivy said everyone usually wanted a tooth; these were turned into necklaces and worshiped as idols. But Sivy did not want a tooth.

When the family had collected the bones, they rinsed them in a colander with bottled water. And since there wasn't much bottled water in the village, the tradition for cremated bones to be rinsed only with pure water showed special respect—though the well water would do for daily drinking and cooking needs.

Sivy's uncle, the only living child of her grandma, placed the bones in a small jar and sealed it. Sivy wasn't sure what he would do with the jar, and she did not remember what had happened to her parents' remains. She also made several comparisons between her father's and grandmother's funerals. She had shaved her head at her father's but not at her grandmother's. And her father was burned in the yard, not in the temple.

The way Sivy interacted with her extended family amazed me. Everything about her showed respect and love for them: her smile, her laugh, her tears, her stance, her listening ears, and her gentle touch.

But never did she compromise her faith. As others chanted, she lifted her eyes to the Lord and prayed. Her presence filled the village with Christ's love. Each time she shared her faith, she brought them hope. God got all the credit for the changes in her life and her circumstances. I saw God use this special child to draw both villagers and me closer to him. And I am eternally thankful.

After the funeral, Sivy, her sisters, her aunts, and I all slept on the floor of the house under mosquito nets. I was uncomfortable; but I was so exhausted I slept well.

After a breakfast the next morning of instant coffee, brown rice, fried baby frogs, and pork, Sivy's uncle asked her to help him write a letter in English to his friend in America.

As a boy, he had lived with a lady for a while, before Pol Pot invaded Phnom Penh. She had escaped the country shortly after the invasion in 1975. As I realized I was sitting with a living history book, he composed a letter to a long-lost Cambodian "sister," who was fortunate enough to have escaped the horrors of Pol Pot. Sivy's uncle knew the woman now had two daughters, who were both doing well, because they'd married Americans. He told his Cambodian friend that he was healthy but poor. And he expressed happy memories of his childhood with her.

Sivy already was serving her people in a special way, each time God used her gifts, although she didn't realize it. Every day was an English lesson!

We finished the letter, and I was overdue for a trip to the bathroom, so I managed the squat-pot toilet in the outhouse and was thankful for the packet of tissues I constantly kept in my pocket. Then since I really wanted to freshen up, I carried a basin of water to a small, concrete ledge behind the outhouse. And though it was littered with old flowers and paper and plastic bags, I set down my Clinique® face wash, toner, and cream. What a contrast they made! But the familiar routine of washing my face brought contentment for the moment.

I took many pictures of Sivy interacting with aunts and sisters as everyone gathered around the table—under the house—for meals. I enjoyed the spirited laughter, even though I could not understand a word. Sivy was having way too much fun to take time to translate. So I simply smiled and watched as they filled their bowls with favorite foods, which had been cooked in my honor.

I did my best to eat a little bit of each thing. But the most difficult things for me were the interesting selections of meats: fried dog in red pepper, cow intestines, beef lung, fried pork skin with hair still attached, and chopped chicken on the bone, including heads and feet.

Barely the day before, I had seen the pork drying, uncovered on a tree branch. Along with all the relatives, the flies were having a great time. I prayed continually for God to protect my stomach and immune system. And though my stomach was far from full, my heart was warm as I watched Sivy enjoy it all! She joyfully expressed that the best part of coming home to the village was sharing food around the table with her family.

Sivy's mother had thirteen brothers and sisters. Six of these aunts and one uncle still lived in her village. After their grandmother's death, Sivy's two sisters planned to move back into the family home. Her married sister, Rachana, and her husband would take over farming the family rice fields. Her engaged sister, Rachany, who had recently trusted Christ, said she would leave her job in Phnom Penh at the garment factory and help with Rachana's little baby and the house. The simple village life would go on, supported by family. My prayer is that Rachany's faith will grow.

"Lord, help Rachany in her newfound faith to understand the emptiness of the pagan rituals. Turn her heart to you and your Word. Help her to see that the beauty of the Cambodian countryside is your creation and a gift. Thank you, Lord, for giving me a glimpse of your plan for Sivy. Her willingness to share brought the Gospel to this village."

I loved hearing Sivy laugh with her sisters and befriend the village children, especially with M&M candies. She enjoyed previous patterns of living, like washing her clothes at the pump and tying her hair back with a piece of straw. She was a confident guide as she led me out into the bushes—in the middle of the night—and shooed the neighbor's pigs out of her yard. We toured the rice fields.

"Look as far as we can see, at the fields and palm trees, and cows. This is my Cambodia!"

Sivy was at home in her village. When her brother asked her to stay at his house in a nearby town, with a bathroom and electricity, she was quick to refuse politely, which I understood.

"I want to be here. This is home," she said.

After visiting in the village for a day and a half, I began to realize the multitude of adjustments Sivy had made when she moved to the orphanage in Phnom Penh and then in with us in Chiang Mai. There among her family, she truly did not see their poverty, hardship, or litter. She saw only their beauty, strength, and determination.

After lunch, I needed time to think and pray, so I took another walk to the rice fields. I had far too much to absorb. When I stopped to rest, a little girl ran across the field in front of me, picking yellow wildflowers. I immediately felt déjà vu, like watching my sweet Sivy as a younger child. I remembered all the little girls in school uniforms, with shiny black ponytails hanging down their backs, riding bikes along dirt paths, on their way to school. Bit-by-bit, God was giving me an understanding of Sivy's past.

Still in the village one afternoon, Sivy asked me to walk with her. She wanted to visit all her aunts and give money to the special ones who had helped her in the past. Each aunt welcomed her warmly, and each responded to us in a similar way. Their eyes welled with tears of greeting as they grasped her hands and respectfully acknowledged me also. They smiled and talked. Then each reached down to touch Sivy's knee, where she still has a large scar, but the disease is gone. Sivy eagerly shared how God healed her knee and left a scar as a reminder of His faithfulness. Many asked her why she was still dark-skinned after so long. They thought she would turn white like her foreign mother!

Often, if a child was around during our visits, the aunt would push the little one toward me and tell the child to go with me, to have a new mother and a better life. Sivy explained that sometimes this was a joke—but not always. These ladies also wanted more opportunities for their children.

When the sun began to lower in the sky, Sivy's sisters started preparing dinner, so she and I headed to the pump for our evening "bath." It didn't matter to us that it was only twenty feet from the house and barely ten feet more from the main road, in clear view of all the relatives who still hung around the yard.

So I became the evening's entertainment. *The large, white foreigner was bathing!* I thought, amused at how we must look. So we laughed along with everyone else. I never would have imagined myself wrapped in a sarong, bathing in cold water, at an outdoor pump. But here I was!

Sivy patiently watched as I tried to get the sarong wrapped around me and secured. Then I had to wiggle out of my clothes and drop them to my feet. When I finally was wearing only the sarong, I ladled buckets of cold water over my body and wrap as she squatted, poised and graceful—a beautiful picture. Then I wobbled around, trying to get my bottom planted on the concrete ledge. It was not a pretty sight, but I laughed along with most of the villagers, who were secretly watching.

Then, since they had no towels, I was given another sarong, a dry one to exchange for the wet one. After another aerobic period of fearful gymnastics to exchange sarongs, I climbed the ladder into the house and dressed in Western clothes by candlelight—sure the village would talk and laugh about the fat, white foreigner for many weeks.

Watching Sivy interact with her two sisters was a real gift. I often saw them sit side-by-side, in deep conversation. Then minutes later, they would erupt in laughter! Both Rachany and Sivy showered Rachana's baby with attention and affection. And as I watched them all work together cooking and washing dishes and clothes, it was obvious they had been happy little girls together.

One day they opened an old box of their mother's skirts and fancy blouses that had been packed away. They put on a "style show," and I took lots of pictures. They were so happy being together, enjoying this simple activity. After seeing all three sisters together like this, I realized how painful the separation must have felt when Sivy left for the orphanage. I can't imagine their agony when she moved to Thailand with us.

We slept under mosquito nets on the floor of the house each night. Sivy's sister Rachana, the baby, and several aunts slept with us. The men were under the house in hammocks.

Then came our final morning, when we awoke before dawn, to start our trip back to Phnom Penh. Rachany boiled water and brought it to me so that I could have coffee and warm water to wash. What a servant. She was so much like Sivy, and I was humbled again.

Chapter 25

Walk Where Sophie Walked

RACHANY CAME WITH us to Phnom Penh. I enjoyed treating her to several days of living in a hotel and more time with her little sister.

When we arrived, we went directly to the orphanage. Again, everyone was glad to see Sivy, and she was asked to speak during their church worship service. And though I'm not sure what she said, she held everyone's attention. She confidently held the microphone and spoke directly into their hearts, with eyes alive and full of love. Even today, she can be in a room packed with people and make everyone feel special.

I also invited Sophie's older sister, Somphor to stay a night with us in the Phnom Penh hotel. Not long before, she had been frustrated with her life at the orphanage and had left to live on her own, supported by a job in another orphanage for HIV-positive children. The position was without pay, but it provided her room and board.

At this Christian orphanage, the basic needs of the children were met, and there was an obvious attempt to keep the facility clean. But badly stained walls, cracked floors, and broken toys revealed the surface of their desperate needs. And my heart was heavy, because Somphor also quit school when she left the orphanage. Where else would she ever find a job to support herself?

I asked Somphor to take me to the part of town where she and Sophie had lived before the orphanage; she agreed. We rode for about thirty minutes, out to the edge of Phnom Penh. Then we turned off the road onto an alley that was lined with garbage, garbage wagons, and the children who pushed them. They collected trash on the streets at night. Many small shacks backed up to concrete walls. No one had running water. Instead, a large, clay pot sat between several shacks and served as the water supply. Babies swung in hammocks inside dark doorways, while stray dogs scrounged through any available refuse.

Sophie's aunt recognized me immediately and greeted me with much excitement. She hadn't expected us, but she was glad to see both Somphor and me. We followed her to a small, one-room shack, where she lived with her husband, three children, and mother. The dark room was without windows or ventilation of any kind. I took pictures for my daughter and told the aunt that Sophie was well and growing. I left a picture of Sophie with her and a small amount of money.

How had my little Cambodian princess ever survived in this squalor? They needed much more than the few dollars I'd left. Again, I felt helpless.

Sophie's aunt said the children here didn't go to school because it was too far away. When I saw the woman's complacency, I gave God thanks for Sophie's strong will and emotional fervor. Her feisty spirit had indeed kept her alive. But my heart broke as I turned to leave, knowing this cycle of poverty will continue, until the children are educated.

Then I walked the dump. I wanted to experience Sophie's playground first-hand. And I got what I wanted, but not without a price. Mountains of garbage stretched as far as I could see. Smells of the smoldering refuse and open sewage dripped through the garbage at my feet, which crushed broken glass, like the entire scene crushed my spirit, until I wept. This was no playground; it was a gateway to hell.

Pathways crisscrossed the mountains of garbage, where little children regularly traveled with their bare feet. They climbed and slid through the filth, oblivious to their surroundings. I wept again, because they knew nothing else.

Over a far mountain of total depravity, three bright-colored kites flew. Each kite string was held by a child at play. *No child should even know this exists*, I thought. And yet, they play in it. I never will watch another kite fly without praying for the child clutching the string.

I was emotionally and mentally broken. These children's situation was hopeless. Then I remembered how God had saved Sophie. Nothing is hopeless for the Almighty. If he did it once, he could do it again.

Chapter 26

The Truth Sets You Free

I PUT ALL the pictures from our trip to Cambodia into a little folder on our living room coffee table. Sophie had seen the pictures of my trip with Sivy to visit her aunt and cousins, including the one of the new baby boy. I don't remember her saying very much about the photos except, "They are very poor, Mom."

One evening, I came home from a teachers' meeting at school, and Paul greeted me with concern. "I think something is bothering Sophie."

She was in bed, so I went up to say "goodnight" and pray. She smiled, glad to see me. We hugged and prayed like we often do, and then her little face turned sad.

"Daddy thinks I lied."

I quickly got to the bottom of the misunderstanding, which concerned Sivy writing a thank you note. I assured her that we did not think she was lying. "You have never lied to Mom or Dad. You always tell us the truth."

As soon as those words were out of my mouth, her face dropped. That beautiful little face clearly revealed shame and guilt. I reached for her hands; she let me hold them.

Then she looked at me and began, "Yes, I lied. I told a big one."

I assured her that no lie could ever make me love her any less. But now she needed to tell me the truth. She asked if I would promise not to tell Daddy.

"No. But I can promise that I won't tell him tonight."

She agreed. Then she went to her nightstand and brought me the album of pictures from Sivy's and my recent trip to Cambodia. She flipped through it until she found the picture of her aunt. She looked at it for several seconds, then said, "This is my mother."

Her big brown eyes remained steady on mine, waiting for a response. But I was so stunned, I almost couldn't speak. This was impossible! We were petitioning to adopt the child on the basis that she was an orphan. It simply couldn't be true that she had a living mother!

Eventually I recovered my thoughts and found my voice. "No, Sophie! That is your aunt. Your mother died when you were little. This aunt took care of you like a mother, and that is why you are confused."

"No. This is my mother."

"But I have a paper from the orphanage stating that your parents are both dead. How can this be your mother?"

"When they took me to the orphanage, they told me to lie. My uncle took me; he told them my parents were dead. They told me if I lied about it, I would have a better life and nicer place to live."

This was all too difficult to believe. And although I was reeling from my own emotions, I didn't want her to carry the pain of this secret alone. So I questioned her further about her biological parents. And the more she shared, the more I knew she was telling the truth.

She remembered her biological dad had many tattoos. Later, he divorced her mother. She remembered he had many friends and was "popular with the ladies." He soon had a new wife; Sophie called her "mother number two." This woman had a little boy about Sophie's age.

Then her biological father got a se cond divorce, and she had "mother number three." All the while, her biological mother still lived near the dump with three children.

During this time, Sophie was passed back and forth between her biological parents. She remembered her biological mother later visited her only once during the five years she lived at the orphanage.

Then I cradled my precious girl like a baby, and we both cried. I stroked her beautiful, dark hair. I wanted so much to carry all the pain for her, but I knew she needed to feel it and grow through it, in order to heal.

As we looked closely again at her biological mother's picture, she talked about how hard her life had been. Then she said, "If my mother would have had soap and shampoo and creams, I think she would have been pretty."

I assured her that her biological mother did have beautiful features, and Sophie had inherited many of them. She talked about her mother's decision to send her to the orphanage, because there was never enough food or a bed for her to sleep in. When her uncle took her away, he had lied that the orphanage had a big swimming pool and many pretty dresses. So when they arrived and found it wasn't true, she wept. There were absolutely no pretty dresses, and there certainly was no swimming pool.

As Sophie continued to talk, I held her, and we both cried repeatedly. I prayed for God to let me carry some of her pain. And again and again, I assured her I never would leave her or send her away.

When she finally realized the truth was exposed, and her life's story no longer included being an orphan, she had a deep concern. "What do I say when people ask me about my biological mother? The principal at school will think I am a liar. What do I tell the kids at school?"

"When you are ready to talk about your mother, you tell the truth. When you don't want to talk about it, you don't have to talk about it. You say, 'I don't want to talk about it now.'"

Then Paul came to her room, to see what we were doing for so long. But when he first entered, Sophie's expression froze. She looked deep into my eyes for assurance.

I looked at her with love and nodded my head, "Yes." Then I silently prayed as she shared her story and the truth with her daddy. What a beautiful moment it was when I saw my little girl wrapped in forgiveness in her daddy's strong arms.

Several days later, Sophie and I went into God's Word and reread the story of Rahab in Joshua 2. Rahab also had told a lie. Was the lie right? No. But in Hebrews, Rahab is called righteous and faithful. We talked about how God knows our hearts and always will cleanse us whiter than snow.

Later, I felt dumbfounded, when I realized I didn't know what it might mean to our adoption petition, since Sophie's mother was alive! So I found the original paperwork that the orphanage had given me when the girls came to live with us. It was all written in Khmer, so Sivy had to translate.

All along, I had assumed that the paperwork verified Sophie's mother was dead. However, much to our surprise, it actually stated that Sophie's mother merely had relinquished her to the orphanage. And since it was a legal document, Sophie did qualify as an orphan, eligible for adoption. She had been left at the orphanage at age five, filled with fear and disappointment, pain and loneliness, not knowing who to trust or where to turn.

In Sophie's words:

> When I was about five years old, my aunt and uncle came to visit us. My uncle told me about a place with a big swimming pool. He said that if I went to live there, I would get lots of new dresses. He also told that to my older sister, Somphor. We were so excited; we didn't think; and we believed him. My mom, step-father, and uncle knew they had to make up a story we would believe. But my sister and I did not know they were lying.
>
> My aunt, uncle, sister, and I took a taxi to the "place" with the swimming pool. My mom did not stop us, because she couldn't take

care of us anymore. When we got there, it was the total opposite. We never got to say "goodbye" to our mom.

I did not feel mad or sad or angry or anything. It was just the way it was.

Chapter 27

Cambodian Adoption

ON FEBRUARY 29, 2007, the phone rang; it was the director of the orphanage in Cambodia. He said we needed to be in Phnom Penh the next day, to sign the adoption papers. We had only three hours notice before we had to get on an airplane, leave Chiang Mai, and land in Cambodia. So we made quick phone calls, packed suitcases, said prayers, and left home. We had waited so long for this day that it was hard to believe that it was happening!

We arrived in Phnom Penh on the morning of March 1, 2007. We checked into the same locally-owned hotel where we had stayed on our previous trip—not because we liked it, but because we knew where it was.

The girls were now eleven and fifteen, both with the beautiful glow of innocence. Paul and I held their hands tightly, as if trying to form a wall of protection around them. The light of their presence seemed to make everything around us darker than I remembered. And I felt a deep, nagging fear that the adoption would fall through, but I prayed fervently for God to help me resist its terror.

We checked into the hotel, then walked down the filthy, crowded street, trying to find a public phone. Broken sidewalks were cluttered with motorcycles and parts of motorcycles, just as before. Piles of garbage attracted flies, where little children looked for refuse treasures. We ignored hollering tuk-tuk drivers, trying to persuade us to ride in their vehicles. Sophie insisted that I give money to help each beggar who carried a baby, and I could not refuse her. Every time I looked into the eyes of a child begging, I saw my little princess, Sophie.

After walking several city blocks, we found a young man sitting at a small booth, selling minutes on a cell phone. Sivy made the phone call to the director of the orphanage, and he told her that the adoption had been postponed until the following day. God took my hand and touched my heart, reminding me that he was in control and that my faith must be in him. "Wait," he said. And thankfully, I was able to listen.

On the phone, the orphanage director also told us to meet him and a friend named Chang in our hotel lobby that same day, for last-minute instructions. We found that Chang spoke English well and did all the interpreting.

First they asked us for the remaining money owed for the adoption. They explained it was customary for adoptive parents to give them a monetary gift, thanking them for handling the adoption process. Next, they added that they also expected us to donate cash to the orphanage. Then they explained that we also would have to pay the fees for the adoption certificates the following day. Finally, Chang and the director left, and we confirmed the official adoption was scheduled for the next morning, March 2, 2007, at 8 A.M.

Later that evening, Sophie's sister Somphor joined us for dinner. The girls ate their favorite meal called "eggs-baby-duck," which is boiled duck eggs, containing developed embryos. Paul and I didn't share their tastes, but we sat in the hammocks of the open air restaurant and enjoyed their smiles.

The restaurant was dirty; the music was too loud; beggars were frequent; yet the evening was good. And though their smiles were sweet to see and their laughter good to hear, this final reunion between Somphor and Sophie was bittersweet. It was clear Sophie was gradually losing her Khmer language, so their conversations were more limited than before. They cherished embraces, because they understood they'd never again live as sisters.

Sivy told Somphor that at our home in Thailand, Sophie had shared the secret truth about their mother being alive.

"Are your parents mad?"

Sophie clung to me for reassurance at Somphor's shock. Sophie wasn't sure Sivy had done the right thing to tell, so I held her tightly and answered simply, "The truth will set you free."

Then she relaxed in my arms and accepted God's promise.

After dinner, Sophie and Somphor rode a dilapidated carnival ride, and we walked along the river. Then we headed to the other orphanage, where Somphor now lived and worked, housed in an old hospital. Sixty children called it home. They ranged in age from two years old to twelve.

The little children clung to us during our visit; each one wanted to be hugged. So I held as many as I could. We took walks down the hall and played patty-cake. It's wonderful that there is no such thing as a language barrier to a two-year-old who just wants to be held.

Later I found Sivy with four little children in one of the rooms at the end of the hall. They were all about five or six years old. Sivy was singing praise songs with them, and the children knew all the words and motions. Pure worship and child-like faith filled that room.

Then Sivy opened her Khmer Bible and began to read in the language of their hearts. The children focused and listened. God filled that room with pure joy as Sivy shared Christ, deeply and easily. He empowers her, and she gives hope and encouragement to those around her. I will always vividly remember the special way she turned that hospital room, filled with little HIV-inflicted orphans, into a sanctuary.

The next morning, we went to an old government building at 8 A.M. It was a dirty site, with paint peeling off the walls. Taped to the wall hung a wonderful paper sign: "Adoption Bureau." So we knew we were in the right place.

We climbed a dirty, uneven set of stairs at the back the building. Then we entered a room that was partitioned with a large book shelf, dividing the office area from the waiting room, where we sat to wait. After only about fifteen minutes on plastic chairs, Chang informed us that the adoption ceremony and signing of all the papers was again postponed, but only until 10 A.M.

Culture shock was closing in on me. All I wanted was a comfortable Western atmosphere and a cup of coffee. I felt like the scum and confusion covering this city was suffocating me. Yet I had to control every expression on my face. I had to remain calm and confident for our girls. I was determined to be respectful and submissive to the government officials until we finished this process.

Since we had only two hours to wait, we headed for the Foreign Correspondence Club on the river front. It was a Western oasis with big leather chairs, a beautiful view of the Mekong River, slowly turning fans, and great coffee. We waited until a little before 10 A.M., then went back to the government building.

Everything seemed to be in order, so Paul and I were called into the office area to sign papers and pay another fee. The girls each had all ten fingerprints taken and printed on the adoption documents. Then we had a group photo taken with the orphanage director and government officials. And finally, they said the process was done. But as everyone was preparing to leave, we realized we had been given no physical documents! Where was our paperwork?

As politely as possible, we asked when we would have documentation of the adoptions. Chang offered to deliver it to us tomorrow, but there would be an additional fee to translate the paperwork into English—of course. So again, we waited.

The following morning, Chang came to the hotel with official adoption certificates for both girls. But he had a birth certificate only for Sopheak, which had been produced in October of 2006. Unfortunately, he said the director of the orphanage had not been able to find a birth certificate for Sivy. In fact, as we discussed it, we realized perhaps there had never been one. But he said a new one could be made.

Birth certificates in Cambodia do not hold the same value as they do in the States. Officials simply reproduce them, stamp them with a government seal, and sign them! So—for another small fee—a birth certificate was made for Sivy. It was not on the same kind of paper as Sophie's, but it did have a government seal and signature.

By 6 P.M. that night, we felt confident that the adoptions were finally, totally, legally done! All the papers were translated and in our hands. So we packed our suitcases and walked down the street to a nicer hotel and checked in. I needed to feel safer, cleaner, and complete tonight.

Somphor joined us again, and we all went to see Sivy's sister Rachany and her new husband. What a blessing they are! He is a strong Christian, who works as a mechanic at the orphanage where he was raised. They live simply, in a tiny, rented room with a small bathroom, a wooden plank bed, a cook burner, and a plastic stand for dishes. But we were pleased to notice several well-worn Bibles stacked at the head of their bed. Christian neighbors came to visit for a while, and we all prayed together. This man, it seems, was the answer to my prayers. He is the one needed to help Rachany in her fledgling faith.

Over the weekend, Sophie asked us to adopt Somphor too. The answer to that question breaks my heart. But Somphor is now a young adult, not eligible for adoption. She made the choice to leave the orphanage and start a life working and living on her own.

"Lord, protect her and keep her strong in her faith. May she follow you all her days."

A yearning to return home to Thailand soon washed over me. I had never been as homesick as I was that Sunday morning. And though I certainly was thankful for everything the Lord had done to complete the adoptions, the "peace that passes all understanding" did not engulf me until I was on the airplane.

Chapter 28

Girls Give Praise

SIVY WROTE THE following note in our March 2007 prayer letter:

> Jesus said, "Ask and it will be given to you." This is true because you prayed, and now I am adopted by the Jarot family. Thank you so much for your powerful and effective prayers.
>
> The Cambodian government said I am a "legal daughter" to the Jarots, but I don't have any special feeling from the words, "legal daughter." All my excitement, thrill, and happiness come from remembering when I first came to live with them, because I knew that they were my parents on that first day. It is not the words "legal daughter" that makes me their daughter. Jesus gave me to them to be their daughter. Living with my parents is such a blessing to me.
>
> Many times, I have jokingly debated with my mom. I thought I was more blessed than she was, because I had new parents who loved me so much and had everything I needed. My mom said she was more blessed because she has me living with her, and she is the one who provides.
>
> At church, I opened my Bible to Acts 20:35, and the red words said, "It is more blessed to give than to receive." I gave the verse to my mom,

and we smiled at each other. I gave up the debate with her because Jesus told me clearly that the one who gives receives more blessing.

Now that I am adopted, I am thankful. The sad part was seeing hundreds of orphans and poor kids in Cambodia who want and need a loving, Christian family like mine. They walk and sleep in the street every day; no one sets their eyes on them. These kids are waiting for someone to love them and provide for them.

The adoption was a big miracle for us and for many other people. Jesus is such an awesome God.

Then Sophie wrote:

Thank you for praying for us! The government's office was nowhere near as fancy as I thought. I thought the walls would be painted nicely, the stairs would have ribbons going around the railings, and the room would be bigger. The couch was uncomfortable, because when you sat on it, you could feel the frame, and it hurt.

The government man put all of my fingers in the ink and pressed them on the paper. I was sooooooo happy because I had blue fingers!

We went to visit the orphanage where my sister works. Most kids made fun of me because I couldn't speak Khmer very well, but my English is much, much better. They don't know how it feels to speak two languages. It makes me feel proud to learn so much.

God bless you!

Chapter 29

Mountains of Paperwork

LEGALLY, THE GIRLS still had their Cambodian names, Sivy Meas and Sopheak Chheang. But more importantly, as far as the government in Cambodia was concerned, they were our daughters. I knew that the United States government never would recognize the Cambodian adoption, but I started the research on obtaining immigrant visas anyway, so they might someday enter America and become citizens.

My daughter-in-law recommended a good immigration lawyer in the Chicago area, so we contacted him. Through him, I learned that the next step was to complete the I-130 form for Homeland Security. This form is required, to prove that the Cambodian adoption was legal and that we were not trafficking the girls. I consulted the Homeland Security website and discovered something else new:

> Children being adopted abroad must be found eligible for adoption under the U.S. Immigration and Nationality Act (I.N.A.) in order to immigrate. Because adoption laws vary from country to country, it is sometimes possible to adopt a child abroad who does not qualify for immigration under U.S. law; such children cannot immigrate to the United States.

> Under the I.N.A., a child who is adopted abroad while under 16, and who has been in the legal custody, and has resided with, his or her adoptive parent(s) for at least two years may immigrate to the United States just like the biological child of a U.S. citizen: he or she may be the beneficiary of a U.S. Citizenship and Immigration Services (U.S.C.I.S.) I-130 petition (Petition for Alien Relative) and receive an immigrant visa in the IR-2 category. Most adoptive parents, however, are unable to spend two years abroad living with the child. (http://adoption.state.gov/visas.html)

When I found and read this, I was more than pleased. The girls had indeed been living with us for more than two years, and we lived overseas. So we packed copies of our marriage license, all four birth certificates, adoption certificates, and all school and medical records since the day of their arrival and mailed them to the lawyer.

He sent them, along with the I-130 form, directly to Homeland Security in Bangkok. It was August, 2007.

We received a phone call from Homeland Security early in September and were instructed to come to the Homeland Security office in Bangkok, to present the documents in person, and to bring the girls with us. We totally expected at that appointment, when we turned in the forms and wrote a check for fees, our questions would be addressed and answered. But that did not happen.

The Homeland Security office is in a large, newly-constructed building with a grand entryway. It is professionally landscaped and clean; security is tight. We seemed to be the only ones there as we rang the bell. An efficient secretary appeared and simply accepted our paperwork. But no other explanations were given. When I asked if we could talk to someone, to answer our questions about the next steps in the procedure, she replied succinctly, "No. We will contact you."

Paul and I left, having accomplished our task but frustrated. We wanted help; we wanted to proceed quickly. We knew our case was unique; we were working against the calendar. Sivy's Cambodian adoption had occurred only five weeks before her sixteenth birthday. And to qualify for an immigrant visa as an internationally adopted child of a US citizen, she had to have lived with us for two years and still be under eighteen.

Even under the best of circumstances, if the Cambodian adoption was accepted by the US Department of Homeland Security without question, we barely would meet the time frame required by our government. We explained to the girls that our job now was to pray and wait. So, we went home to Chiang Mai.

Several weeks later, Homeland Security called and said our paperwork was not in order. They said we had no evidence of legal guardianship before the adoption. To be granted an alien relationship, the child has to have lived with the legal guardian for two years. Our petition was not granted—but neither was it denied.

They instructed us to reapply on March 3, 2009, because we did not yet meet the requirement of a two-year legal guardianship relationship. It appeared that the US government considered our legal guardianship to have started on the day the Cambodian adoptions were completed, on March 2, 2007.

This gave me hope, but to a greater degree, it also threw me into a panic. We had to get the "I-130 Petition for Alien Relative" form approved before Sivy turned eighteen. But we could not submit the form until March 3, 2009, and her eighteenth birthday was barely one month after that, on April 7.

So, although we had already spent a large sum of money on this first attempt toward immigrant visas, we'd learned a lot, but we weren't finished. Over the next fifteen months, I prepared for the next I-130 Petition for Alien Relative. This time, I was determined to complete it correctly, and without the expense of a lawyer—so I had mountains of paperwork and many sleepless nights ahead!

And all the while, my life was full of the normal routines of being "Mom," the responsibilities of being a wife and a school teacher, plus the added burden of new paperwork for an international adoption.

I was on "overload," but there was nothing I could let go. My faithful husband prayed and took on many household jobs so that I could continue with the adoption paperwork. Our lives were indeed challenged, full, and blessed in the most unusual ways.

Chapter 30

And the Tears Fell

MEANWHILE, SOPHIE HAD brought two pet hamsters into our home. She loved them, even through their messes and foul smell. And she was absolutely sure they were both girls, because they were so "cute." One was white and the other light brown.

And though I did not want these animals, we allowed Sophie to buy them with her own money. I thought it would be a good way to teach responsibility and management of her allowance. She had to purchase all their food and wood chips for the cage. So our growing family now included a dog and two hairy hamsters.

One day, as I came home after teaching half-day kindergarten, I let Polly, the dog, in through the back door. But to my great surprise, the neighbor's cat was also in the house! In an instant, our dog was chasing the cat from room to room. Eventually, I caught the dog and put her outside, then returned to find the cat.

After I cornered it in my closet, I talked quietly and sweetly as I lifted it, because I was afraid of getting scratched. Then as quickly and gently as I could, I tossed it out the door. It would have to deal with Polly on its own as it ran home.

But as I went back inside the house, I also saw wood chips on the stairs. This was not a good sign. I followed the trail into Sophie's room and there discovered the destruction. Her hamsters' cage was on the floor—open. Her beloved China doll that had stood on the dresser next to the cage was broken all over the floor. And her hairy cuties were gone.

At first, I hoped I could find them and catch them for her. But after I cleaned up the mess in her bedroom, I went into the downstairs bathroom and found blood smeared on the floor. It appeared that the neighbor's cat had had lunch.

When Sophie came home from school later, I told her the sad news. And of course, she cried.

Then she wailed, mad at the world. "I should never have bought the hamsters. If they were still at the pet market, they would be alive!"

She accepted the loss, and an uneventful week passed. Then the pain returned and erupted into a fit. As she cried this time, she talked about not being understood by anyone and crawled under her bed to get away from even me. So I crawled under the bed with her. But in her anger, she fought and pushed me away. But I did not leave.

I prayed aloud, and eventually, she let me hold her. As we embraced, I rocked her, which I often did to sooth her emotional outbursts. Then she opened up and explained her pain—but only after I promised to listen and not talk. Sophie had lived with rejection and separation in many ways, and the death of another pet simply brought her feelings to the surface again.

She asked, "Can my biological mom live in our sewing room? If she had a shower with shampoo and some body lotion, she would feel better and have a better life."

I listened without talking, and we wept together. The reality of separation from her biological mother was still painful. I love Sophie so much. And God continues to heal my little girl from the inside, while also strengthening me.

Many days, I did not feel strong at all, not up to the task of parenting all over again. I felt small and inadequate. But I was so deeply thankful for these two girls. Our lives were much richer since they came, but I often asked God why he chose me to mother them. There are many hundreds and thousands of younger women, trained as counselors, with experience in the issues of adopted adolescents. But God's clear answer to me is always the same: "Walk close to me and trust me."

So I continued to step forward, one day at a time, trusting that he will be there when the next tears fall.

Not long after that, Sivy and I began attending a mother-daughter Bible study on the book of Daniel. Our lessons included a video series from the instructor. It was excellent, and we both looked forward to it every week.

One week the study led to the discussion of living in today's "Babylon" with integrity and without following the ways of the world. The instructor shared her personal struggles of how she had overcome sexual abuse from her past.

When we got home that evening, Sivy came into my room, laid on the bed, and quietly put her arm around me. "Mommy, those bad things happened to me too. Am I pure in Jesus' eyes?"

Almost instantly, like a burst dam, my tears fell. I had prayed never to hear those words from my daughters. Especially not from both of my girls! But now my precious Sivy had shared her secret pain too.

Sivy had known her abuser. So after a few weeks, she called him and confronted his past acts. In her heart, she longed to forgive him, and she told him so on the phone as she cried. But we both knew that healing from this kind of wound would take a long time. And over the years, I have watched in true, amazed wonder as God's peace and forgiveness have cleansed and healed my little girls.

My pain needed an outlet. My neatly-structured world did not have a place to store the grievous sin that was just revealed. I picked up a pen and wrote to my girls:

Forgiveness, it heals and refreshes
I seek it and receive it from Christ
But not without pain

I must forgive even when the offense was not directed at me
Pain goes deep and breaks my heart:
"Does Jesus still see me as pure?"
Pain that deep quickly becomes anger
Forgiveness is stronger than the pain, the anger, the sin
But only through Christ
Tears, hugs, time, and phone calls all work together toward forgiveness
Forgiveness, it heals and refreshes
But not without pain

Chapter 31

Community of Prayer

MARCH 3RD WAS always nagging in the back of my mind. It was the day I needed to reapply to Homeland Security for approval of the Alien Relative Petition. So I organized a portfolio for each girl that included all their paperwork from Cambodia and its translated copies, birth certificates, adoption certificates, and photocopies of their Cambodian passports.

Next I checked all their medical and dental records, from their first pediatrician visits to their current immunization records. Then came all paid receipts for their school fees and report cards. Finally, I included all of their academic and sports awards.

We had to prove we were parenting these girls, and we were grateful that Homeland Security did its job of double-checking every document. To stop child trafficking, the government must be thorough in its investigations.

By January of 2009, I had our forms and portfolios completed and called Homeland Security in Bangkok with a few important questions: "Do I have to start over with all the original documents for the I-130 form?" "What is the next step after I get the approval from Homeland Security?" "Is there any way to expedite the process?" "When do the girls become citizens?" "Are there any more fees after the application for the immigrant visa?"

I called several times and talked to anyone who would listen to my story. I knew I was under pressure to do everything right, because we had no time to waste. We totally understood we had one shot at this. And if I missed, Sophie would be able to apply for US immigration as an internationally adopted child—but Sivy *never* would.

Eventually, I got two clear answers. I found that I indeed had to start everything from the beginning, with all the paperwork and original documents for the I-130 form. But regarding the next step in the process, I was told we would no longer work with the Homeland Security department. Now I needed to contact the State Department instead, to inquire about immigration visas.

So I searched the Internet and read everything about international adoptions and immigration on the official US State Department website. But the more I read, the more confused I got. There are so many laws that I did not understand, plus hundreds of different forms. And because our case was unique, our situation did not seem to fit any of their forms.

Though I felt totally overwhelmed, I kept reading, until I eventually found a phone number. Now I could call with my questions, and I had plenty of them! But the voice at the other end was on a machine. So I followed the instructions and pressed buttons to different offices for about three minutes. And finally, after a long wait, I heard a real person on the other end, to hear my first and most pressing question: "How long does it take to process the I-130 Relative Alien Petition form?"

"Six months. We send them to the USA for approval. Then the forms are returned to our embassy in Bangkok. When they arrive, we will notify you. Then you can apply for an immigrant visa."

"Six months! I don't have six months. I don't even have six weeks."

The pressure of our timeline was mounting at home also, but I did not realize how much. Sivy said that she was fine with the idea of Sophie immigrating as an internationally adopted child, even if she could not.

She was always so proud of her Cambodian heritage. But I did not realize what stress this might put on her.

Now it seemed that every conversation, every day around the dinner table ended with discussion of the immigrant visa process. Sivy struggled with her fears, but she was not able to verbalize them.

Then one night at about midnight, she knocked on our bedroom door. "Mommy, I can't breathe!"

I had no idea what was wrong, so I took her temperature. It was normal. I gave her a drink, and we prayed together. She seemed fine for a few minutes, and then the labored breathing started again.

This time, her pleading eyes filled with tears. "Take me to a doctor."

We were out the door within minutes! I drove her to the emergency room at the hospital. They admitted her immediately and took her vital signs. Everything was normal—except for the fear in her eyes. As she labored to breathe, I held her hand. The doctor came in and explained there were no airway obstructions, and all of her vital signs were strong. She seemed to be suffering from an anxiety attack. He gave her medication to help her relax and also sent some home with us.

Later, I called my dear friend and counselor, and she lovingly talked and listened to Sivy. We all realized this was an experience to grow through, so Sivy did not take any more medication.

About that time, we shared our adoption and immigration story at church, and many prayed for our "paperwork" situation. Then one Sunday after church, a man greeted us and said he might be able to help. He had a friend with a connection in the State Department. He asked if I would be willing to share our story with that person, and I eagerly accepted.

Several days later, he sent an email, instructing me to share our story with his contact at the State Department. I wrote to her right away and explained why we needed help to expedite the immigration process because of Sivy's age. I explained we lived in Chiang Mai and wanted to fly to the US and stay only long enough to complete the girls' citizenship requirements and get their US passports. I also asked what the next step was after the I-130 Alien Relative Petition.

The woman from the State Department replied and answered each question carefully. She promised to watch for our case to cross her desk and make a note of the need for its expedition.

The State Department also explained that once Homeland Security approved the I-130 Alien Relative Petition form, we would be invited to apply for an immigrant visa on the basis that the girls were now our "legal alien relatives." The specific instructions would be revealed to us when we received the invitation. At this point, all we knew was that we had to travel to Bangkok, turn in the I-130, and wait again!

Finally, I was encouraged, because I'd gained some understanding of the process. But I knew that only the Lord could orchestrate the timing to get it done in the thirty-seven days before Sivy's eighteenth birthday.

Chapter 32

Forms and More Forms

PAUL BOUGHT TICKETS to Bangkok, and we made reservations to stay at a guest house. Almost obsessed with searching the government website, I continued to gain as much information on the requirements for immigrant visas as I could. We learned that the girls needed complete medical exams, and Sivy needed a police clearance from Thailand.

So we tried to get the medical exams done in Chiang Mai, before our appointment on March 3rd in Bangkok. But we discovered the exams had to be recorded on "special" medical forms, which I could not receive until I had the immigration application. And I could not get that application until the I-130 was approved.

Now I was totally frustrated with emails and websites, so I made an appointment to speak to a counselor at the US Embassy in Bangkok, on the afternoon of March 3rd. I basically wanted to talk to a real person!

So I packed a large briefcase with the girls' original birth certificates, copies of all the documents we had given to Homeland Security, both girls' portfolios, and copies of Paul's and my birth certificates and marriage license.

We flew together to Bangkok and were waiting at the Homeland Security Office as soon as they opened. We presented the completed I-130 forms, along with a cover letter explaining the need for expedition. They received it politely, and we left. There was nothing else to do.

After lunch, we went through security and into the US Embassy for our scheduled appointment. When our number was called, I walked to the window and introduced myself.

But I had barely begun to explain our story when the secretary interrupted me. "Oh, Mrs. Jarot, we have been expecting you. Have you turned in the I-130 to Homeland Security?"

"Yes, first thing this morning."

"We have not yet received word of the approval. But here is your immigration packet. It includes the application and all the medical forms you will need. There are also instructions on how to get a police clearance, since Sivy is over sixteen. You need to get started."

I left the embassy with tears of joy. God had gone before us. Friends and family all over the world were lifting us in prayer, and we felt God's leading.

We got a taxi and headed to the police department. And though we had a bit of confusion because of our limited Thai language skills, we finally found the "Police Clearance Division."

Sivy filled out more forms, had her picture taken, and was fingerprinted. We paid the requested fee and asked to have the results by the end of the week. A pleasant female officer said her supervisor certainly could do that for us and directed us to his desk. There we filled out another form and were told to return at the end of the week—a few steps closer!

Everyone enjoyed dinner at a nice restaurant near the guest house, and then we all retired for the night. I was exhausted, but I knew I had to read the instructions for the immigrant visa application and begin filling it out. And it was a good thing I had brought all the extra copies of certificates and legal documents, because I was starting a paper trail all over again. We had to reproduce every single document and then more, including financial records to prove our yearly income. Thankfully, we had a copy of our W-2s, so we included them.

The next morning, we were off to the hospital with the proper medical forms. Both girls had physicals and were pronounced healthy. They received two more immunizations, and then we left with sealed envelopes that needed to be submitted with their immigration applications.

From the hospital, we taxied back to our embassy to turn in the completed visa applications and medical forms.

The same secretary met me at the window again and reviewed the applications. But when she reviewed our financial page she exclaimed, "Oh! Your income is below the lowest standard for immigration. You fall into the poverty level, according to US standards. I'm sorry. You do not have enough income to support these children in the United States; therefore, they do not qualify for immigrant status."

I could not believe what I'd heard. We had been pursuing this adoption for more than two years, and we had never even heard of an income requirement. Was it all going to be denied based on that alone? We had lived well on our missionary salaries for ten years in Thailand, and we planned to continue living in Thailand, until the Lord directed us elsewhere.

I tried desperately to explain that, but she did not understand. So she left to get the counselor general. The counselor already had looked at our case and remarked that it was indeed unique. He was firm but pleasant and instructed me to get copies of all our assets. He also wanted a copy of our past year's tax return.

We had to find a legal way to show our income was over the poverty level. If not, our only alternative would be to complete another form and have a friend or relative in the States be responsible for the girls' financial needs, should we ever be delinquent. Smiling on the outside and crying on the inside, I picked up all our paperwork and left the embassy.

The taxi ride back to the guest house was somber, but Paul prayed and assured me that God was not finished yet. We would trust Him for the next step.

First, we contacted our tax accountant in the States, and he faxed our tax returns. Next, we called the head of our mission organization, and he sent a letter stating that we were in good financial standing and had the required financial support needed to provide for a family of four living in Thailand. Third, we spoke with the accountant at Grace International School. He wrote a letter adding to our income level the cost-value of our girls' free tuition (since we both taught there), plus the cost-value of our teacher-free school lunches. Finally, we had our state-side real estate agent fax a letter, showing the value of our small cabin and property in Wisconsin.

Then we taxied back to the embassy in Bangkok to submit the added paperwork. We became quite familiar with the security personnel and procedures. We found the long periods of waiting on plastic chairs gave us time to relax and pray.

When our number was called, we submitted the additional paperwork at the window. The counselor accepted it, reviewed the total, and assured us we surpassed the poverty level. We left rejoicing and headed back to the guest house. That evening, we all got a good night's sleep!

The next morning, we taxied to the police headquarters to pick up Sivy's clearance. After we registered, an officer asked Paul, Sophie, and me to sit in a small waiting area. He led Sivy over to a desk for a private interview. We saw only her back as she talked with an officer.

Then he handed her the papers to sign, but she refused. He continued to talk with her, though we could not hear their discussion. Then Sivy turned to me, and I saw she was crying!

I rose from my chair to go to her, but I was stopped by another police officer. So Paul stood and started toward her.

"It is OK, Daddy; I will do this," she said.

Paul and I were furious, because it was clear she was distressed. But we did not know why. She eventually signed the papers and received her police clearance. The woman police officer who had helped us previously, now escorted us out of the office.

"They told me I had to sign a paper that said I did not pay for this police clearance, but I knew that we did. They took money from us the last time we were here. I finally signed it, because I did not give them the money; you did."

Then I cried with her. We had walked into the "gift" trap, without knowing what we were doing. We had no idea, when they previously asked us for money, that it was not part of the standard procedure. I thanked God we were past this step and prayed for the Lord's forgiveness of my anger and for his continued protection.

Chapter 33

The Whole Truth

AFTER ANOTHER TAXI ride and more security checks, we were back at the US Embassy, waiting on plastic chairs again. It felt like this day of appointments would never end.

But this time when we were called to the window, we were legally sworn-in: "Do you promise to tell the truth, the whole truth, and nothing but the truth, so help you God?"

"Yes."

"Did you apply for immigrant visas?"

"Yes."

"Do you know what it means to immigrate to the US?"

"Yes. It means that our girls can move to the US and apply for citizenship."

"Are you planning to move to the US? Tell the whole truth!"

"We plan to go to the US for a short period of time, just long enough to get the girls' citizenship and passports. Then we want to return to Thailand. Our home and jobs are in Thailand. But we work for an organization based out of the US."

"Do you have a valid driver's license in the US?"

"Yes."

"Do you have a bank account in the US?"

"Yes."

"Did you vote in the last election?"

"Yes."

The counselor gave a reassuring nod and then turned his computer screen around. On it was the email I had sent to the woman at the State Department, explaining our plans to enter the US, get citizenship and passports, and return to Thailand.

"I understand your situation and that you do not have much time before Sivy's eighteenth birthday. But before I let this go forward, I want to build a strong case."

He typed a bit more on the computer, and then turned the screen toward us once again and directed his next question to the girls, "Do you know the man on this screen?"

"Yes. He is the director of the orphanage where we lived in Cambodia," they both answered, almost in unison.

Paul and I looked at each other and read each other's thoughts. *How did he get that picture?*

The counselor looked directly at Sivy and asked, "Do you know that his last name is the same as yours?"

"Yes. Meas is a common name in Cambodia, but we are not related."

The counselor accepted her answer, and then explained he wanted to check on the Cambodian adoption and make sure it was legal. He contacted the American ambassador in Phnom Penh, Cambodia, and instructed him to provide verification of our adoption through the Cambodian government.

By this time, we had been in Bangkok four days, and the embassy soon would be closed over the weekend. The counselor suggested that Paul take the girls home to Chiang Mai, so they would not miss any more school. He said I could stay and finish the paperwork.

The counselor reiterated that he wanted a strong case to support these immigrant visas. Then the girls were sworn-in one more time and had their official interview, before they left with Paul.

When I was finally alone in Bangkok, I prayed. And Sunday night, I attended a worship service at a guest house. After the meeting, a young woman asked me, "Are you Paula Jarot?"

"Yes."

"It's so good to see you again. I am Astrid, Martin's sister-in-law. We met at his wedding in Cambodia."

What an answer to another prayer! I now had a friend to pray with and spend the weekend with as I waited for the embassy's decision. We ate together, laughed, and prayed. Fellowship among believers is always an exceptional blessing.

Then on Monday morning, I was back at the embassy. The Cambodian adoption had been investigated and cleared as legal. However, the next hurdle was bigger than anything I could have imagined. They needed an original birth certificate for Sivy—and her mother's death certificate.

The birth certificate we had received when the adoption was finalized in Cambodia appeared to be a copy; yet the original might be available. But Sivy's mother had died in their village and was cremated at the local temple.

I had been to a funeral at that same temple. I'd watched relatives pick through the remains and choose teeth for necklaces. How could I ever obtain an original death certificate? We were running out of time, and now it looked as if I was on my way back to Cambodia, to find both a birth and death certificate.

The counselor explained that the Family Record Book we had turned in as part of Sivy's paperwork had her mother's birth date listed but not her death. So according to our Record Book, her mother was still alive! So now the burden of proof fell on Sivy.

"My mother is dead. Sophie's is not," she cried on the phone. "Why do I have to prove this?"

I just let her cry. When she finally dried her tears, she started making contacts. First she called the director of the orphanage. Next she called her brother, who still lived near the village. She explained the situation and what she needed from each of them. They assured us that they would do their best, and we all prayed. Then I bought plane tickets to Cambodia.

I landed in Phnom Penh late on a Wednesday night; my return ticket was for Thursday night. I had to get the required certificates back to the US Embassy before they closed on Friday. And I had only one contact number of an English-speaker, who was employed at the orphanage. I made the initial contact and left my hotel phone number. I waited; I prayed.

Sivy's brother contacted the local government office in his province, quickly working to obtain a death certificate. The orphanage director searched for an official birth certificate. Then Thursday afternoon, a thrilling phone call informed me that both documents were ready!

I gingerly hopped onto the back of a motorcycle-taxi and rode to an official translator, paid for a rush translation, and headed for the airport and my plane back to Thailand. All the paperwork looked official to me, but I would not know the outcome until everything was examined by the United States Government officials at our embassy.

By Friday morning, I was back in a Bangkok taxi, hurling through rush-hour traffic and praying fervently that all the paperwork was in order. In addition to photocopies, I still was carrying all the girls' original documents and guarding them with my life.

The embassy security guards greeted me with a friendly smile; then I found a seat on my favorite plastic chair. When my number was called, I went to the window—almost holding my breath—and presented the final original birth and death certificates.

As the counselor glanced over them, he said they looked in perfect order. But he needed time to review everything again and asked me to return at 3 P.M. So I left the building, carefully crossed the busy street to the Homeland Security Building, drank a fruit shake, prayed, and tried to relax.

At three o'clock, I again greeted the security guards, carrying my "legal file cabinet," and found "my" plastic chair. All the other people in the waiting room were Thai. And they also were applying for their immigrant visas.

The woman next to me gave me a questioning look and spoke in careful English. "Why are you here? Aren't you an American?"

All I could answer was, "Yes."

At last my number was called. Nervous with excitement, I carried everything to the counter.

"Mrs. Jarot, everything is in order. I am happy to issue immigrant visas to your daughters."

Then all my emotions, disappointments, and prayers that had built up over the past four-and-a-half years exploded. I wept without control! In the middle of my dam-burst, I repeatedly, profusely blubbered our thanks to the counselor. But because I literally was shaking with absolute joy, I dropped my files all over the floor. The counselor graciously came from behind the glass and helped me. Then I gave him a big bear hug, knowing—at that moment—God had given us a miracle! Praise the Lord! What a mighty work he had done!

On March 20, 2009, Sivy Meas and Sopheak Chheang received immigrant visas to the United States of America.

Five days later, we were on our way to Hawaii. We had barely eighteen days until Sivy's eighteenth birthday. And though we were all emotionally and physically drained by the international adoption process, when we landed at the Honolulu airport, we finally could see the end of this journey.

I had been told we should go through immigration and then proceed to a special counter for adopted children. I was under the impression that the certificates of US citizenship would be issued at the immigration department at the airport. But once again, I was wrong.

Chapter 34

Run the Race

WE SLOWLY MOVED through the line labeled "Immigration" as each person's passport was stamped. At our turn, I asked, "Where do we go to get the certificates of citizenship?"

"I don't do that here. It's not my job."

"Can you tell me where I go to get the certificates?" By this time, my head began to throb, and I felt I could lose my composure.

"You have to go to the Immigration Office."

"Can you please tell me where the Immigration Office is located?"

"No, I don't know where it is. Look it up in the phone book."

I was talking to an immigration officer at the airport! How could this person not know where the Immigration Office was? I grabbed a tissue to wipe my eyes, forced a smile, and prayed for patience. Then I continued to ask for help. "I don't have a phone book with me; I do not even have a cell phone that works in this country. I am very tired. Could you please check the Internet on your computer for the address of the Immigration Office?"

"Go over there," the officer said with a grunt, pointing to a nearby counter.

We were pleasantly assisted by an airport employee, who gladly "Googled" information on the Immigration Office and printed an address for us. Again, we were on our way.

Thirty minutes later, we arrived at the Honolulu Immigration office. I took a number; we waited in line. When we were called to the window, the agent said I could *not* speak to anyone, because I did not have an appointment. And the only way to make an appointment was to use a computer across the room.

At that moment, I felt and probably looked totally frazzled. And as I turned to look where that specific computer screen was located, I simply burst into tears. How would I know what selections to make? What buttons to push?

So I called Sivy over to me, and she walked me through the process, figuring it out as we went. Our appointment was now scheduled for the following day.

When we were in the States the previous summer, we had shared our adoption story at a Sunday night service in a small Wisconsin church. As we concluded the story, we had asked for prayer for the immigrant visas and for traveling to Hawaii. It was important for us to enter the United States at the Honolulu airport only, because immigration was especially prepared there to process Asian adoptions. We'd explained that this port of entry was the quickest way to complete the immigration before Sivy's eighteenth birthday, but we had no idea where we would stay.

After the prayer, Chick and Sharon Stults graciously had offered their beautiful home in Hawaii for us to use. So, fortunately, we had a home to rest in for three weeks as we completed the final paperwork. We were blessed with both Christian fellowship and luxurious accommodations.

The first night, when we were all together, Paul started our prayer time by asking Sophie what she wanted to pray for.

She looked out the window at the water, the boat, the pool, and then inside the home at the big-screen TV and dishwasher. "I pray that I don't get used to living like this!"

But brutal reality would hit us hard again the next day, when we walked into the Immigration Office. It was good that we'd all had a deep night's sleep and felt the world was a better place. When my number was called, and I went to the window and inquired about the certificates of citizenship, I was handed two more forms to complete—and charged another large fee.

The girls still had their Cambodian last names, but we all agreed we wanted them to have our name, Jarot, on their citizenship papers. So when the first question on the official form asked for the "name," I did not know which one to use.

So I asked a clerk for help and explained the situation. But much to my surprise, I was told that staff absolutely could not give any help. And If I made a mistake, the application would be totally rejected, and we would have to start over again.

They certainly didn't understand we had no time to start over! The girls' legal names were Meas and Chheang, but we wanted it changed, so what should I write?

I prayed, wrote "Jarot," and turned in the application.

I exchanged friendly smiles with the woman behind the glass, who said, "We will call you."

So we left the building and went to the pool to wait.

On April 1, 2009, we received a phone call, asking us to return to the Immigration Office. When we entered, officials led us to an office behind their public windows. Numerous agents shuffled their chairs around to make sure everyone had a seat. The presiding officer was pleasant and commented that she usually did not do this with "older" children.

On her desk I saw all our forms, everything that I had meticulously completed from the very beginning of our immigration process. Each piece of paper and every document had followed us here. Sivy's stack was approximately four inches high, and Sophie's was two inches thick. The officer looked at the girls, opened the first file, and asked, "These girls are from Cambodia?"

"Yes."

"What adoption agency did you use?"

"We did not use one."

"Did you have a lawyer?"

"No."

"Then who did all this paperwork?"

"I did."

Then she pushed back her chair and removed her glasses before continuing. "How did you get these girls out of Cambodia and into the United States?"

Before I could answer, Paul asked, "Do you want to hear the whole story?"

"Yes, I want to hear the whole story from the beginning."

"Twenty-three years ago," I began, "we were on our way to Papua New Guinea as missionaries. We stopped in Hawaii, because the P.N.G. Embassy had lost our passports. We met a man named Tom Patrick there."

The women sat spellbound as I continued to share the complete miracle of these two Cambodian girls.

"So now we are back in Hawaii, awaiting the approval of the girls' citizenship," I eventually concluded.

She smiled and declared, "That was faith!" Then she picked up her black "APPROVED" stamp and firmly pressed it onto every document that we had accumulated for the past two years.

Within an hour, copies of their United States citizenship were printed and in their hands. The girls' legal names were now officially, legally, and happily Sivy Jarot and Sopheak Jarot.

And they were United States citizens—six days before Sivy's eighteenth birthday deadline!

Lawyers, a judge, adoption agencies, embassies, and two national governments had clearly declined our requests: "No. Legal adoption and immigration of these two older girls is not at all possible, ever!"

But God had a different plan. He knew these girls were to be our daughters—our daughters by *his* design!

Epilogue

EIGHTEEN MONTHS AFTER the girls received their United States citizenship, my journal was transcribed into the manuscript of this book, *Daughters by Design*. But before I sent it to the publisher, I wanted to read it aloud to Paul and the girls. They knew nothing would be published without their consent. So we drove up into the mountains and checked into a beautiful resort for a three-day family retreat.

The girls and I cuddled into a king-sized bed, and Paul sat across from us in a comfortable chair. We were together, and it felt safe. I afforded a silent praise and started to read: "They came without suitcases…"

Both girls drew closer and read over my shoulder. This was *their* story, and they were eager to hear how it would sound to the world. I knew some of the memories still were painful, and tears often welled in my eyes as I read. Each chapter brought memories to the surface, and as a family, we needed to experience the joyful laughter and cleansing tears of each memory—before it went to print.

Sophie was often quick to interrupt and say, "Really? I don't remember that!" When she had come to Thailand about six years before, she did not remember talking to her sister about being separated or the opportunity of an education being so valuable. She did remember crying but could not remember why. Then her face lit up when I called her my Cambodian Princess in the book.

Halfway through the book, Sivy said, "Mom, the story is mostly about Sophie, but that is all right."

I quickly explained that when they arrived, Sophie was very animated and full of antics, while she was quiet and observing. "Just wait. Your story is coming," I assured her.

Sivy stopped my reading several times, with great suggestions for more details, so I took notes. She helped rearrange a sentence or two, in order to sequence every phrase precisely. And when difficult memories brought us tears, we all cuddled closer, and I looked into their eyes for assurance to continue. But Sivy and Sophie both prompted me to continue.

The more I read, the stronger the bond grew among all four of us. We relived our entire journey again and were amazed anew at the many miracles. Then, as I read the final sentence, I was reassured that God had indeed designed our unique family. And I am forever grateful that God did not let me say, "No," to that possibility.

About the Author

Paula Jarot chooses first to be known as a woman of God; and then as a dedicated wife and the mother of three biological sons, Christopher, Michael, and Nathan, and two adopted Cambodian girls, Sivy and Sophie—so beautifully described in this story; and last as a loving teacher.

She and her husband, Paul, have shared a faithful missionary journey overseas, entirely guided by God's direction since 1986. They first worked in Papua New Guinea, and then they assisted in the development of a much needed missionary school in Chiang Mai, Thailand.

Their boys were raised in the mountains of Papua New Guinea, along with local native boy Bizo. Both Paul and Paula have dedicated most of their adult lives to teaching missionary children, integrating basic educational skills with a Christian worldview perspective.

Contact Information

To order additional copies of this book, please visit
www.redemption-press.com.
Also available on Amazon.com and BarnesandNoble.com
Or by calling toll free 1-844-2REDEEM.